Ralph Ellison in Progress

Ralph Ellison
in Progress

From *Invisible Man* to
Three Days Before the Shooting . . .

ADAM BRADLEY

Yale

UNIVERSITY

PRESS

New Haven and London

Published with assistance from the foundation established in
memory of Philip Hamilton McMillan of the Class of 1894,
Yale College.

Set in Minion type by Integrated Publishing Solutions,
Grand Rapids, Michigan.
Printed in the United States of America by Maple-Vail.

Library of Congress Cataloging-in-Publication Data

Bradley, Adam.
Ralph Ellison in progress : from Invisible man to Three days before
the shooting . . . / Adam Bradley.
        p.   cm.
Includes bibliographical references and index.
ISBN 978-0-300-14713-1 (alk. paper)
1. Ellison, Ralph—Technique.   2. Ellison, Ralph—Manuscripts.
3. Ellison, Ralph. Invisible man.   4. Ellison, Ralph. Three days
before the shooting . . .   I. Title.
PS3555.L625Z57   2010
813'.54—dc22   2009036607

A catalogue record for this book is available from
the British Library.

This paper meets the requirements of ANSI/NISO Z39.48−1992
(Permanence of Paper).

10 9 8 7 6 5 4 3 2 1

To John F. Callahan
On the *Higher* Frequencies

Contents

Ralph Ellison in Progress

Introduction
1993

Ralph Ellison's untitled second novel ends—or rather, it stops—when its protagonist, Alonzo Zuber Hickman, takes a "quick look at the glowing 369 on the fanlight" as he hurries away from the startling scene he has just witnessed at an old townhouse somewhere in the nation's capital. Saved to his computer in December 1993, just months before his death in April 1994, these are among the final words of fiction Ellison would write.

As far as last words go, they seem like something of a disappointment. After all, they do not complete the novel Ellison had been laboring on for more than forty years. They do not sum up his life in letters; they offer no tidy epitaph. Yet for those initiated into Ellison's literary fellowship, they provide a fitting, if profane, bookend to his career as a novelist.

The secret lies in the number. Three-six-nine. You'll recall from *Invisible Man*'s prologue that Ellison's unnamed protagonist illuminates his underground hideaway with a vast number of lightbulbs. "In my hole in the basement," he gleefully explains, "there are exactly 1,369 lights. I've wired the en-

tire ceiling, every inch of it." This inscrutable detail has per-
plexed readers since the novel's publication in 1952, at least
those curious enough to linger over Ellison's unusual numeric
specificity. Perhaps the numbers held a coded meaning. Perhaps, some suggested, he chose 1,369 because its square root is
thirty-seven, Ellison's age when he published *Invisible Man*. Ellison remained coy on the matter.[1]

An alternate interpretation of the digits can be found
among the numbers runners and payday gamblers in Ellison's
Harlem. The numbers racket, also known as policy, was an off-
the-books lottery where players would select a number, usually
three digits long, in advance of a drawing. Claude McKay, writing in the mid-1930s, just before Ellison arrived in Harlem,
notes the wild popularity of policy. "As the game gripped
the imagination of the Harlem masses," he recalls, "the business of numbers magic flourished. Negroes became canny
about numbers. Any number seen, or which came to one's
mind under unusual circumstances, would be played." Few
numbers were as infamous for policy players as three-six-nine,
a numeric combination with its roots in Southern hoodoo.
Blues lyrics, like these from Blind Arthur Blake's "Policy Blues"
from 1930, warn against the number's potency:

> I acted the fool and played on 3, 6, 9
> I act the fool and played on 3, 6, 9
> Lost my money and that gal of mine.[2]

Often players would draw their numbers from dreams,
and the means of translating dreams into digits was a dream
book, those numerological tomes that match anything your
subconscious can conjure with a number ready to wager. In-

visible Man finds such a "great constitutional dream book" among the belongings of the evicted elderly couple in Harlem. Mary Rambo consults a dream book in one of the novel's expurgated drafts. For anyone familiar with a Harlem dream book, the meaning of Ellison's number would have been clear. Just as six-nine-four stands for rabbit and four-three-five stands for raccoon, three-six-nine stands for excrement.

That Ellison places this numerical inside joke both at the beginning of *Invisible Man* and at the end of the second novel offers an unexpected symmetry, a small gesture toward a greater truth. Ellison's fiction is united by this spirit of play, his unabashed embrace of folk idioms alongside the rarified literary culture he worked hard to claim. The reappearance of that funky coded number at the end of Ellison's literary life suggests the value of a backward glance. Heeding Invisible Man's admonition, perhaps Ellison had come to believe that for his fiction "the end is in the beginning and lies far ahead."

Although critics tend to look to the beginning of Ellison's life—his childhood and adolescence, his formative artistic experiences, his passion for music—as a means of understanding his artistic maturity, this book offers something different: a backward glance at Ellison's fiction from the perspective of his final, unfinished novel. Reading both novels in the process of their becoming endows us, like Ellison's nameless protagonist from *Invisible Man*, with a "slightly different sense of time." "Sometimes you're ahead and sometimes behind," he explains. "Instead of the swift and imperceptible flowing of time, you are aware of its nodes, those points where time stands still or from which it leaps ahead. And you slip into the breaks and look around." This book is structured on such nodes of time in Ellison's life and literature. Beginning in the 1990s with his last efforts to complete the second novel, it moves backward through critical moments of stasis and transformation, moments of standing still and leaping ahead.[3]

Interpreting *Invisible Man* in the same way as the manuscripts of Ellison's second novel reveals them both as works in progress. Instead of definitively settling matters of plot, character, and perspective—a necessary task for the author when preparing a novel for publication—such a critical approach opens them back up, not with the idea of second-guessing the author, nor even of suggesting that the published novel might stand to gain by the addition of this expurgated material; rather, the purpose is to expose the discrete textual decisions and indecisions that escape our view when reading the published novel alone. The result is a living text whose protean forms underscore the necessary indeterminacy of the artistic process.

Ellison's numerous manuscript drafts and notes housed in the Library of Congress constitute an evolving record of his aesthetic vision. The provisional, often fleeting nature of these working drafts charges them with a force undiminished by time. Unlike a published novel, which is the product of its author's acts of formal limitation as well as creation, these manuscripts in progress retain a sense of unfettered possibility. In Ellison's drafts, Invisible Man can have a wife, or not; Sunraider can die, or somehow live on; first-person narration can take the place of third-person, or both can coexist alongside each other without the necessity of resolution. Ellison's second novel gives us no choice but to confront such compositional complexity. The unfinished novel is defined in large part by the choices Ellison did not make, the discrepancies he left unresolved. To read *Invisible Man* in the same open-ended manner is to participate in an act of critical imagination.

I've written this book because I believe that we stand to gain by reading *Invisible Man* as we read Ellison's novel in progress, opening up settled matters of novelistic judgment so as better to comprehend Ellison's two works of fiction and his career as a whole—the classic novel published in the first half of his life, and the unfinished novel never published in the second. My own experience coediting *Three Days Before the Shooting . . . : The Unfinished Second Novel,* the Modern Library edition of manuscripts from Ellison's second novel, along with Ellison's literary executor, John Callahan, shapes my conviction that Ellison's second novel is the best means by which to measure Ellison's literary legacy, *Invisible Man* included, for the twenty-first century. For more than a decade I've had the privilege of studying closely what Ellison wrote in the last forty years of his life. I've seen Ellison as few have to this point—in his flights of inspiration and in his moments of obvious exhaustion, as he gloried in his own virtuosity and as his estimable powers of craft began to fail him. This book represents the fruits of my study.

To read Ralph Ellison in progress is to come to terms with the seeming paradox embodied in his compositional method: as Ellison himself once put it, he was a fast writer but a slow worker. In other words, although he often composed with ease and fluidity, he constructed his fiction with painstaking deliberation. "The problem," Ellison told John Hersey, "is one of being able to receive from my work that sense of tension, that sense of high purpose being realized, that keeps me going. This is a crazy area that I don't understand—none of the Freudian explanations seem adequate." Ellison's distinction between slow working and fast writing sheds some light on how he could have written thousands of pages for his second novel without ever producing a published volume. Writing, after all, was just part of the craft of fiction; the rest lay in responding to the textual challenges embodied in his own expansive vision. Like his nameless protagonist, Ellison was a "thinker-tinker"; he continued to play with the possibilities of language and theme until the last.[4]

In his theory of artistic creativity, University of Chicago economist David Galenson divides all artists into two classes: conceptualists and experimentalists. Conceptual artists work from highly articulated plans with specific goals in mind; they often produce their best work at a young age. By contrast, experimental artists work incrementally, letting their goals evolve over time to fit the shape of their changing conceptions. Ellison was an experimentalist par excellence. One can read in Galenson's description of the experimental artist something of Ellison's cast of mind.

> The imprecision of their goals means that these artists rarely feel they have succeeded, and their careers are consequently often dominated by the pursuit of a single objective. These artists repeat themselves, painting the same subject many times, and gradually changing its treatment in an experimental process of trial and error. Each work leads to the next, and none is generally privileged over others, so experimental painters rarely make specific preparatory sketches or plans for a painting. They consider the production of a painting as a process of searching, in which they aim to discover the image in the course of making it; they typically believe that learning is a more important goal than making finished paintings. Experimental artists build their

skills gradually over the course of their careers, improving their work slowly over long periods. These artists are perfectionists and are typically plagued by frustration at their inability to achieve their goal.[5]

Ellison fits Galenson's description in most ways. He was a perfectionist driven by high standards of craft and aesthetic purpose. He doggedly pursued a single objective in his fiction. He engaged in seemingly endless repetition over decades, rewriting the same small set of scenes time and again, often with only subtle variations. Paradoxically, he seems both to have reveled in this process and to have grown increasingly frustrated by his inability to publish a second novel.

Understanding Ellison as an experimentalist makes it easier to conceive the second novel's failure but perhaps harder to explain *Invisible Man*'s success—that is, until you recall that *Invisible Man* was nearly seven years in the making and that it took its final shape only after a Herculean exertion of editorial will in the months before publication by Ellison and a host of others, including his editor, Albert Erskine, his wife, Fanny, and a close group of literary conferees that included Stanley Edgar Hyman, Albert Murray, and Harry Ford. By contrast, the second novel was a nearly solitary endeavor, as his circle of confidants steadily diminished until Ellison seems finally to have found himself alone with his computer, in a hermetic isolation of his own creation.

Told in this manner, the story of Ellison's literary life seems like a tragedy: promise unfulfilled, talent dissipated, creativity extinguished too soon. Although such a narrative has the virtue of simplicity, it is finally insufficient. The thousands of pages of notes and drafts Ellison left behind strongly assert a counternarrative that cuts against this tragic arc of his literary career. Ellison's abiding faith in his own work remained, a spark of energy igniting his writing to the last, a blues-toned eloquence that refused to fade. Even as his literary skills gradually diminished in the waning years of his life, his fiction often retained a striking clarity of insight. One ever senses this energy, this sense of an author's work still very much in progress. Such hope as Ellison's late work shows does not brook tragedy—at least it does not allow it without the leavening balance of what Ellison termed "sanity saving comedy." It comes as little surprise, then, that a tragicomic tone predominates in the second novel, particularly in the late years of Ellison's composition. It stands as testimony to his resilience, as well as to his unflagging commitment to the complex spirit of the African-American tradition from which he drew strength. The true story of Ellison's unfinished novel is the same story as that of his literary life as a whole: one of imagination that never yields to despair, even as his last efforts at realizing his grand ambitions proved too little for the time.

Invisible Man was Ellison's masterpiece, but the second novel was his life's work. After all, Invisible Man was a first novel written in Ellison's thirties. It was a powerful statement of aesthetic purpose, the product of hard-earned lessons in the craft of fiction begun in the late 1930s when Ellison started his literary apprenticeship among the writers of the New York Left, and particularly Richard Wright. Even in its supreme achievement, however, Invisible Man bears the telltale marks of a first novel in its occasional infelicities and moments of excess.

By contrast, the second novel as it takes shape over the decades often shows Ellison working at the height of his artistic powers, employing the lessons learned in composing Invisible Man and the texture of experience gained over time.

Where *Invisible Man* improved through tightening its focus, consolidating its voices, and limiting its themes, the second novel gains resonance through broadening, diversifying, and expanding.

Ellison's two novels follow an antiphonal pattern, with *Invisible Man* voicing a call and the second novel's multiple drafts offering an extended polyphonic response. Their relationship suggests both continuity and departure, an expansion of Ellison's literary ambitions nonetheless grounded in familiar themes of identity, democracy, and freedom. To read the manuscripts of Ellison's second novel is, in some ways, to read Ralph Ellison himself in progress. It is to understand that all works of fiction bear the marks of the discrete decisions, sudden improvisations, even the errors their authors make in the process of composition. It is to assert that every novel is also a record of its historical moment. Amoebic in form, Jurassic in size, the second novel shifts shape to fit both an artistic vision and a nation still very much in progress.

The last half of Ellison's life coincided with seismic shifts in American politics and culture, from Jim Crow segregation to the civil rights revolution, from the death of the author to the birth of the digital age. As a consequence, the manuscripts of his second novel embody a rich and sometimes confounding range of experience. Whereas Ellison scrawled his first ideas for the novel in a small composition book, he typed the final lines on a laptop computer. Even as he identified himself as a member of "that Vanished Tribe . . . The American Negro," he never wavered in his insistence that the nation work to perfect its multiracial democracy. His final, unfinished novel is a testament to this proud identity and complex faith. With all its obvious faults and deficiencies, it will never equal *Invisible Man* as a literary achievement, but it may prove even more pertinent to the challenges facing us in the twenty-first century.

The publication of *Three Days Before The Shooting* ... demands that we adjust the center of gravity of Ellison's literary legacy, shifting a greater share of the balance toward the final forty years of his life and the novel that even now, more than a decade after Ellison's death, is emerging from an extended hibernation. Considering Ellison's two novels together, one an American classic, one defiantly unfinished, Ellison's value to our present time proves inescapable and unforgettable.

The absence of a second novel published in Ellison's lifetime is by no means evidence of the absence of his labor. Beginning before the publication of *Invisible Man* and stretching until just months before his death in 1994, Ellison composed thousands of pages of notes, typescripts, and computer drafts. The Library of Congress's Ralph Ellison Archive includes twenty-seven boxes dedicated to the second novel as compared to eleven for *Invisible Man*. Ellison spent more than half his life working in one way or another on his manuscript in progress, living among the same cast of characters, returning to the same core scenes, many of which had taken shape in his imagination in the 1950s.

The plot of the second novel as it emerged over the decades centers on the connection, estrangement, and reconciliation of two characters: a black jazzman-turned-preacher named Alonzo Hickman and a racist "white" New England senator named Adam Sunraider, formerly known as Bliss—a child of indeterminate race whom Hickman has raised from infancy to adolescence. The narrative action concerns Hickman's efforts to stave off Sunraider's assassination at the hands of the Senator's estranged son, a young man named Severen. The narrative follows Hickman from his home in Georgia to the Oklahoma City of his jazz-playing youth to the nation's capital in search of clues that will not only save the senator but also perhaps unlock the mystery of the child Bliss's disappearance decades before and his reemergence as the race-baiting Sunraider, an enemy of the very people who raised him and continue to love him to this day.

In its grand conception, Ellison was writing a novel about betrayal and redemption, love and loss, black and white, fathers and sons. It takes as its theme the very nature of America's democratic promise: to make the nation's practice live up to its principles in the lives of all its citizens, regardless of race, place, or circumstance. In this regard, it is an extension and an amplification of *Invisible Man*—a fitting response to the question that closes the novel: "And it is this which frightens me: Who knows but that, on the lower frequencies, I speak for you?"[6]

Behind this question is Ellison's radical assertion of democratic values: that a young black man can speak not only to, but perhaps for, everyone at a time when segregation was still the law of the land. Ellison understood that freedom first found definition in the imagination. As he would reflect in the introduction to the thirtieth-anniversary edition of *Invisible Man*, "If the ideal of achieving true political equality eludes us in reality—as it continues to do—there is still available that fictional *vision* of an ideal democracy in which the actual combines with the ideal and gives us representations of a state of things in which the highly placed and the lowly, the black and the white, the Northerner and the Southerner, the native-born and the immigrant combine to tell us transcendent truths and possibilities such as those discovered when Mark Twain set Huck and Jim afloat on the raft." Catching upon the metaphor, he expands it into a theory of novelistic expression, an American aesthetic imperative: "Which suggested to me that a novel could be fashioned as a raft of hope, perception and entertainment that might help keep us afloat as we tried to negotiate the snags and whirlpools that mark our nation's vacillating course toward and away from the democratic ideal."[7]

Ellison carried this vision of the novel as a raft of hope over into his work in progress, expanding the contours of its already lofty aims to embrace a direct and active political function for his fiction. "At its best," he explained to John Hersey in 1982, already two decades into composing the second novel, "fiction allows for a summing up. The fiction writer abstracts from the flow of experience certain abiding patterns, and projects those patterns as they affect the lives and consciousness of the characters. So fiction allows for a summing up. It allows for contemplation of the moral significance of human events. . . . It is that aura of summing up, that pause for contemplation of the moral significance of the history we've been through, that I have been reaching for, in my work on this new book." Captured in that redolent phrase, "the aura of summing up," is the very spirit of democratic engagement in fiction, the "speaking for you" that his protagonist puts forward in the last lines of *Invisible Man.* From these conjoined concepts it is possible to define the terms of Ellison's literary ambition: the measure of artistic greatness is the ability to capture the cultural present and preserve it as a living testament for future generations.[8]

Ellison's desire for his novel to embody the spirit of his time, the "aura of summing up," is inextricably bound up in its protracted composition. Had his aspirations not run to the

seemingly unachievable goal of summing up American experience, then he might well have published the book at any
number of points in its composition. Ellison suggests as much
himself. In a 1982 interview he responds with rare candor to a
writer's question about the novel's delay, then already a quar-
ter century long. "Well, writing is a discipline," he began in his
familiar fashion. "It's not important how much you write.
Anyway, part of what's taken so long is that so many things
have changed so fast in our culture that as soon as I thought I
had a draft that brought all of these things together, there
would be another shift and I'd have to go back and revise all
over again." Read alone, this seems more like an excuse than an
explanation, a way of deflecting inquiry. But when set beside
the numerous typescripts, the episodic drafts that make up
computer sequences, the labor of more than forty years, Ellison's meaning becomes apparent.[9]

A novel that began as a study of race and nationality at
the dawn of civil rights era transforms through time into an
implicit account of the movement's victories and defeats, and
finally ends—though it never truly concludes—as a prophetic
meditation on the multiracial American future that we are
even now struggling to achieve. In this last iteration, Ellison
provides at once his most incomplete fictive statement and his
most compelling contribution to some of the great debates
that continue to shape our democracy in the era of Barack
Obama. What is an American? How does racial identity relate
to national identity? What is the way forward in a nation that
all too often fails to exercise its principles in everyday practice?
These questions have always animated Ellison's writing, from
his early efforts at fiction to *Invisible Man* to his essays, but it is
in these expansive, incomplete attempts to capture America in

his second novel that Ellison comes closest to achieving his grand purpose.

For all the thousands of pages of fiction Ellison wrote in the last half of his life, the discussion of Ellison's literary career after *Invisible Man* is most often subsumed in a single question: How could Ellison have written for forty years without completing a second novel? Critics, confidants, and observers have raised and rejected a host of theories. Some cite the 1967 fire at the Ellisons' vacation home in Plainfield, Massachusetts, that saw a summer's worth of revisions go up in flames. Ellison himself seems to support this interpretation at times, often invoking the fire as a defense when asked about the novel's slow progress in the years that followed. Others point to Ellison's growing wariness of publishing a novel that centers on a politician shot on the floor of the Senate in the aftermath of the political assassinations of the late 1960s.[10]

Still others suggest that Ellison made himself too available in public life, both in his service as a lecturer, board member, and educator, as well as in his busy social affairs, commitments they believe left him ill equipped to practice what Ellison termed the "very stern discipline" of fiction. And there are those who posit that Ellison became a victim of his own high standards of literary craft. "Like few other contemporary American novelists, Ellison must feel burdened after having reached the literary summit on the first try," writes Jerry Gafio Watts in perhaps the clearest articulation of this last perspective. "It is an intimidating experience to live to see your first novel become a classic before you are able to publish your second. His already exacting standards when coupled with the burden of attempting to match or surpass *Invisible Man* have added to the difficulty of completing a second novel." Watts even ascribes to Ellison "a rather extraordinary if not potentially self-destructive bid for excellence" as the explanation for the second novel's long delay. But, as I shall demonstrate in the chapters that follow, Ellison was grappling with writerly conflicts, not psychological ones. In reading the numerous drafts of the second novel and the attendant working notes, one gleans little of this sense of psychological burden but a great deal of concern for the practical challenges of craft.[11]

The impulse to seek explanations in his personal life for Ellison's failure to publish a second novel is both a sign of critical exhaustion and, at least in part, an understandable consequence of the dearth of published material from the book. Ellison published only eight excerpts in his lifetime, and the posthumous release in 1999 of *Juneteenth* provided what John Callahan called "the most ambitious, latest, freestanding, compelling extended fiction in the saga." At 348 pages, however, *Juneteenth* represented only a fraction of the work-in-progress. Now with the publication of *Three Days Before the Shooting . . .* , scholars and general readers alike may seek answers to their questions in the fiction itself. So much newly available material obviates the need for speculation. The answers are in the fiction itself; the challenge lies in finding them within a series of overlapping manuscripts that are often taxing to critical attention.[12]

Perhaps the most surprising evasion of Ellison second novel comes in Arnold Rampersad's *Ralph Ellison: A Biography*. In his otherwise meticulous consideration of Ellison's life and literature, Rampersad gives scant attention to the thousands of pages Ellison wrote for the second novel. He telescopes the last three decades of Ellison's life, the most prolific period of the second novel's composition, into only five chapters out of a total of twenty-one. When Rampersad does discuss the second novel, it is almost always in extraliterary terms—as "The Monkey on His Back," in the words of one chapter title, or as an occasion to psychoanalyze Ellison's motives. Through correspondence, Rampersad chronicles Ellison's shifting emotional responses to his novel. He goes to great lengths to suggest that Ellison made too much out of what he lost in the Plainfield fire, using it as an excuse for his failure to finish.

More striking than what Rampersad's biography includes about the second novel, however, is what it does not. Nowhere does Rampersad attempt to reconstruct the stages of the second novel's composition, explore the central themes, or provide any more than a perfunctory description of its plot and characters. Nowhere does he note that Ellison became one of the first major authors to adopt the personal computer as his primary means of composition. Nowhere does he communicate the idea, so vivid in Ellison's private notes and even in his public interviews, that Ellison considered himself to be writing a novel that would achieve "the aura of summing up," describing the nation to itself in the language of fiction. This palpable sense of aspiration, even if only partly realized—even if failed entirely—merits discussion. It is impossible to understand Ellison's evolution as an author, certainly impossible to engage the question of the second novel's protracted composition, without considering the numerous manuscripts of his novel in progress as they evolved over the decades.

Reading Ellison's manuscripts, it soon becomes apparent that his reasons for not publishing a second novel likely had little to do with psychological disposition, procrastination, or lack of focus and almost entirely to do with his failure to solve certain basic textual challenges presented by his material. For all the writing he did, Ellison had yet to resolve the questions of craft required of fashioning his drafts into a whole. Always bedeviled by transitions, he found himself continually struggling with how best to fit the episodic pieces of his narrative together. Captivated by his quest of "summing up" American experience in a single novel, he was routinely thwarted by the passage of time, which would render his best efforts to capture the historical moment insufficient once that moment had passed. Although Ellison was drawn early on to the antiphonal interplay of Hickman and Bliss, he increasingly found his narrative taken over by Hickman alone. As long as the novel remained in progress, he could comfortably sustain such indeterminacy, could allow for such irreconcilable conflicts within his fiction. Once he made the discrete textual decisions necessary to produce a complete novel, however, the freedom he seems to have found in the open-ended manuscript would have been lost.

Ellison's struggle to master his fiction is played out in the many pages, revisions upon revisions, of his sprawling manuscripts. To spend an afternoon among the papers is to invite the captivation—even the mania—that must have gripped Ellison. For all that is lost by Ellison never having produced a second novel, we have this to gain: a rare glimpse of a literary master at work. Like a jazz musician riffing and improvising but never settling on a final take, Ellison offers the literary equivalent of a great master's complete studio recordings. The experience of reading Ellison's work in progress is so exhilarating, the insights into the artistic mind so profound, the perspective on the nation so raw and poignant, it seems nearly incomprehensible that any serious consideration of Ellison, indeed, any serious consideration of American literature in the second half of the twentieth century, could overlook it.

Ralph Ellison in Progress aims to recapture a sense of Ellison himself in progress, to clarify the hidden name and complex fate of his second novel while complicating settled views on *Invisible Man*, at the same time showing how both novels are bound together in Ellison's singular pursuit of a literary ideal: crafting a novel capable of summing up America, to ourselves and to the world. Departing from the conventional scholarly line on Ellison that considers *Invisible Man* as a kind of premature culmination of his literary career and the last forty years of his life as a sad decline, I argue instead that Ellison's protracted period of composition of his second novel offers invaluable insights into the making of *Invisible Man* and the long trajectory of Ellison's novelistic career. Reading Ellison in progress reorients our critical perspective by allowing us, just as Invisible Man once described, to slip into the breaks and look around.

Part I

I

1982

Ralph Ellison's laptop weighed twenty-five pounds and could, its manufacturer touted, be "safely stowed under the passenger seat of most aircraft."[1] It was an Osborne 1, one of the world's first portable computers, and although it was cumbersome and almost comically feeble by today's standards (it had a paltry 64K of RAM and a five-inch green-text monitor), it was state-of-the-art when Ellison purchased it in 1982. Ellison used it to write letters, store addresses, record stray thoughts, and, most important, continue to compose the novel he had been writing for nearly three decades.

That Ellison would be an early adopter of the computer as a means of composition comes as no surprise. Ever since his boyhood in Oklahoma he had been fascinated by technology, working with short-wave radios and ultimately becoming something of an expert in high-fidelity audio components. He had also taken to using recording devices to capture and play back portions of the second novel read aloud in the seclusion of his study.

Until 1982, however, Ellison's technological tinkering remained a hobby, a pleasant diversion largely removed from the
craft of his fiction. He wrote by hand and by typewriter, en-
listing his wife, Fanny, to retype clean copies that incorporated
his penciled emendations in the margins of his drafts. This
was a time-consuming process, often resulting in overlapping
pages, irregular numbering, and inadvertent omissions and
repetitions. The computer would change all of this, transforming Ellison's compositional method and leaving an indelible mark upon his final manuscript so long in progress. In
the process, Ellison would emerge as arguably the first major
author of the digital age.

In the years between Ellison's acquisition of the Osborne
computer on January 8, 1982, and the last file he saved on December 30, 1993, Ellison amassed a textual archive with a scope
approaching what he had composed of the novel during the
previous three decades. All told, he saved more than 3,000
pages in 469 files on eighty-three disks using three computers.
The files range from single paragraphs to complete episodes,
each labeled by some distinguishing feature of character or
scene. While some files are grouped episodically, many are dis-
persed in no discernable order among the disks. Several partial
tables of contents provide clues to narrative sequence, but Ellison left no comprehensive table that would give definitive
shape to the novel he spent nearly half his life composing.

Together the computer files relating to the novel resem-
ble a kind of high literary jigsaw puzzle. But unlike a child's
game, the various fragments that comprise the manuscript do
not always fit neatly together, nor do all the necessary pieces
exist to make up the whole. This stands in clear contrast to
much of his writing from the 1950s to the 1970s, significant
portions of which he would distill into two lengthy narratives,

which he would label Book I and Book II. Book I comprises the first-person narration of Senator Adam Sunraider's shooting and its aftermath from the perspective of a white newspaper reporter named Welborn McIntyre. Book II, much of which was published in *Juneteenth*, consists of Ellison's third-person rendering of Hickman, and finally, Hickman and the dying Senator exploring the past through conversation, remembrance, and reverie. Whereas Ellison seems to have revised the Book I and II typescripts into clear, if still disconnected, unities, he achieved nothing of the sort with the computer files. Placed alongside Book I and II, the computer sequences read like the unfinished drafts they are: at times wordy and obtuse, at others lyrical and sublime. They call attention to the intensity of Ellison's labors as a novelist, but also to the unevadable fact that much of that labor appears miscalculated and misspent.

Even after the 1999 publication of *Juneteenth*, discussion of the second novel still centers on why Ellison failed to publish the manuscript himself. It has become something of a cottage industry among critics to speculate on its protracted composition. "The novel has to be more than segments, it has to be a whole before it's ready for publication," Ellison told an interviewer in 1982, the year he purchased the Osborne and began the transition from typewriter to computer. Far from a whole, and perhaps still far from a novel, the manuscript as it emerges in the computer files remains a puzzle. The jigsaw complexity of the numerous textual variants and the sheer magnitude of the composition present a paradox: Ellison wrote enough for ten novels, but not enough for one.[2]

Not only was 1982 the year Ellison's made the pivotal shift of composing the second novel from typewriter to computer, it was also the year of the reemergence of *Invisible Man*. To commemorate the thirtieth anniversary of the novel's publication, Random House was preparing a special edition with a new introduction by Ellison. Not surprisingly, Ellison's mind would turn to his classic text, the novel he had wrestled into shape decades earlier. In private notes, he makes overt something he would only hint at in public remarks: that he somehow needed *Invisible Man* as a guide to completing this second novel. He admonishes himself to fit his fiction into the pattern he had drawn long ago from Kenneth Burke, the tragedic progression from purpose to passion to perception. He continually drafted and redrafted outlines of key incidents in the plot, on several occasions even setting side by side the chronologies of his two novels. The challenge he faced was one of giving form to his creation; he had no problem producing pages. "It looks long enough to be a trilogy," he told one interviewer. He continued:

> It all takes place in the 20th century. I'm convinced that I'm working with abiding patterns. The style is somewhat different from *Invisible Man*. There are different riffs in it. Sections of it are publishable and some parts have already appeared . . . .
>
> I'm dealing with a broader range of characters, playing with various linguistic styles. Quite a bit of the book is comic. The background is New York, the South, an imaginary Washington—not quite the world I used to encounter on the board of the Kennedy Center for the performing arts.
>
> The novel has to be more than segments, it has to be a whole before it's ready for publication. But if I'm going to be remembered as a novelist, I'd better produce it soon.[3]

Any discomfort or embarrassment he felt from not publishing the novel was outweighed by his desire to see it through. This new novel, so different from *Invisible Man*, drawing from many voices, many styles, must be of a whole. The computer, it seemed to Ellison, was just the tool he needed. That same year, another interviewer described Ellison at work. "When I arrived," he recalls, "Ellison was editing his novel in progress with a video terminal on a cluttered table in his den." Asked how the work was progressing, Ellison was circumspect: "Coming along fine, thank you." And, by all evidence, it was.[4]

Ellison's shift from typewriter to computer helped stimulate what appears to be a significant flowering of inspiration and a profound change of direction in his fiction. Turning away from Books I and II, which he had honed throughout the 1970s, he returned instead to older typewritten episodic fragments, perhaps from as early as the mid-1950s. These mostly undated early drafts, now housed in the Library of Congress and filed by episode or character name, are about as removed as one can get from the Faulknerian interplay of Hickman and Sunraider at the Senator's bedside from Book II. They deal, instead, with the incidental—from Hickman's encounters on the streets of Washington, D.C., to Sunraider's youthful adventures as a roustabout and hustler. The change is not simply one of content but also one of tone and style; these early drafts are often bawdily humorous where the typescripts are elegiac—they push action outward rather than drawing it in. That Ellison would so emphatically turn away from the more polished typescripts and toward the rawer draft fragments is a significant, if surprising, decision. Over the next decade, it would follow a concomitant move away from Sunraider toward a nearly consuming preoccupation with Hickman, his actions and ruminations. For whatever reason, Ellison was returning to the beginning.

From the mid-1950s, when Ellison first conceived the plot, to the early-1980s, before he took to composing on the computer, it appears that Ellison practiced much the same compositional style as he did with *Invisible Man*. He would jot down notes for characters or scenes on scraps of paper, in bound notebooks, and even on the backs of envelopes. Then he might write longhand riffs that he would integrate into typed drafts. He would take pen or pencil to these typed pages, putting them through scrupulous revisions, often producing half a dozen—even a dozen—drafts until he was satisfied. These episodes would then be rendered in sequence with others until he assembled a continuous narrative, which he would then retype (or have Fanny retype) into a clean copy that he would subject to even more edits. His editor, Albert Erskine, recalls how the two of them read the entire manuscript of *Invisible Man* out loud, with Ellison making subtle—sometimes significant—changes to the text. It appears that he did the same on his own with the second novel, even recording his voice on tape and playing it back to catch small infelicities in the prose.

Until 1982 Ellison's compositional method for his second novel seems like only a grander version of the one he employed in the making of *Invisible Man*. Any difference is one of degree rather than of kind. But something fundamental changed when he began writing on the computer, affecting both his means of composition and the fiction that resulted from it. I believe this change helps explain why the novel's progress seems to have stalled at the very time when Ellison was by all accounts most eager to complete the novel and appeared to have the perfect tool to see it through.

Ellison's second novel did not remain unfinished in the last twelve years of his life for lack of effort. He wrote assiduously, and his rare statements, both public and private, about the book support the textual evidence that he wanted to finish the novel. He must have believed that acquiring a computer would give him just what he needed to accomplish this. Using a computer, he could manipulate his prose in ways unattainable through conventional means, moving entire passages and changing individual words throughout a text with a keystroke. Ellison had found a compositional tool that suited his episodic method of composition and supported his near-obsessive attention to detail.

To illustrate this point, consider Ellison's revisions of what was to be the opening paragraph: Hickman's arrival in Washington, D.C., the beginning of the prologue. Some version of this paragraph exists in the novel's earliest drafts from the 1950s to the first published excerpt from the book, "And Hickman Arrives," from 1960, to the prologue from the 1972 typescripts and to a computer file labeled "Arrival" and dated July 1, 1993. Here are three versions of the opening sentence, from 1960, 1972, and 1993:

> Three days before the shooting a chartered plane-load of Southern Negroes swooped down upon the District of Columbia and attempted to see the Senator. ["And Hickman Arrives," *Noble Savage*]
> Two days before the shooting a chartered plane-load of Southern Negroes swooped down upon the District of Columbia and attempted to see the Senator. [Book I and *Juneteenth*]
> Two days before the bewildering incident a chartered plane-load of those who at that time were po-

litely identified as Southern "Negroes" swooped
down upon Washington's National Airport and dis-
embarked in a confusion of paper bags, suitcases,
and picnic baskets. ["Arrival," computer sequences]

The changes between "And Hickman Arrives" and the typescript are small—only the substitution of two days for three.
But the computer file, the last time Ellison would revisit the
sentence, is markedly different. It displays what will prove to be
the hallmark of Ellison's computer revisions—expansion and
extenuation. He amplifies the sentence with adjectives ("bewildering") and circumlocutions ("what at the time were po-
litely identified as"). He even betrays a certain discomfort with
"Negro," a label long in disrepute by the 1990s, but which he
still used to define himself and his people. Expressing in
thirty-nine words what before had taken just twenty-four, the
sentence is embellished but not improved. This file is only the
last in a series of ten drafts composed on the computer that
variously revise the opening of the prologue. In the first sentence alone, Ellison goes from describing the group as "Southern 'Negroes'" to "'black'" to "Afro-American."

   This spirit of substitution, extenuation, and adornment
extends from the manuscript's syntax to the narrative structure itself. Whereas both previous drafts of the prologue push
the action quickly to the crux of the plot, the Senator's shooting, the computer drafts get caught up in the incidental, following Hickman and his parishioners throughout the day and
halting abruptly, still a day away from the shooting. What is remarkable is not that Ellison found the incidental to be of
interest to him—after all, *Invisible Man* is structured almost
entirely on interrelated incidents—but that he engaged in
near-compulsive revision of the same core group of scenes. Al-

though he certainly revised thoroughly when composing by hand and by typewriter, the extent of these revisions increased markedly with his work on the computer. Indeed, the vast majority of pages Ellison saved to computer are not new scenes but revisions of old ones, sometimes done a decade apart. The complete narrative action of the three computer sequences consists of forty-six files. This means that the remaining 423 files are made up almost entirely of variants of the same material found in the core files. Instead of writing horizontally, connecting the episodes into a cohesive narrative, he seems to have written vertically, stacking draft on draft of the same scene upon one another.

To say that Ellison wrote thousands of pages, therefore, is somewhat deceptive. Ellison always composed by episode, a habit that undoubtedly helped dictate the episodic form taken by *Invisible Man,* a novel one could easily imagine going on indefinitely were it not for the inclusion of a prologue and epilogue to bracket it in narrative time. It seems that Ellison envisioned following a similar structure with his second novel; indeed, he has composed a prologue that sets the scene of the action, establishing a time present. But he never seems to have composed, or even conceived in notes, an epilogue. As a result, it is possible to imagine the episodic sequence continuing indefinitely, to conceive of Ellison writing a novel without end.

Mentioning the scope of Ellison's composition brings to mind such massive tomes as Marcel Proust's seven-volume (three published posthumously) *Remembrance of Things Past* or James Joyce's *Finnegans Wake.* Some have compared Ellison's unpublished manuscript to Robert Musil's 1,744-page posthumously published *Man without Qualities. Three Days Before the Shooting . . .* however, belongs in a category all its own. The most remarkable fact of the second novel is that for all the decades of its composition, thousands of manuscript pages, countless notes, and numerous files saved on computer disk, the entire narrative action would likely take up little more than the space of *Invisible Man.* Books I and II together amount to approximately 650 manuscript pages, and although they do not include every scene Ellison ever conceived, they certainly represent a self-contained literary conception. In revising the novel into these two books, Ellison has made clear compositional decisions, rejecting the alternate visions proposed in variant drafts found in the archive.

That Ellison's second novel remains forever in progress, however, allows for a suspension of these laws of fiction. The same scene can exist in multiple iterations, each maintaining equal authority. In other words, there is really no such thing as a superannuated draft; nothing is ever obsolete because Ellison never made any final judgments, never made the tough decisions that turn a manuscript into a novel. The computer enabled this by creating a "fluid text," one that postponed indefinitely the fixity of a printed manuscript.[5] This is not to suggest, however, that we can draw no critical distinctions among alternate files. Indeed, without imposing a certain critical discretion on Ellison's material it is all but impossible to glean anything of value from it. The material demands that we take on the role of active readers in the fullest sense, cocreators of Ellison's fiction in a way that few novels require or even allow. By shirking these responsibilities we miss the opportunity to experience moments of literary brilliance. We also miss gaining a rare glimpse into the inner workings of a novelist's mind.

The challenge Ellison's literary executor, John Callahan, faced in first editing Ellison's manuscript into publishable form was precisely this—inhabiting Ellison's mind while maintaining a degree of deference and critical remove. *Juneteenth,* in spite of the controversy surrounding its publication, has gained a valued place in Ellison's oeuvre and, indeed, in twentieth-century American literature. Nonetheless, it is an imperfect stand-in for the totality of Ellison's vision and execution, as Callahan was well aware. "Taken all together, the manuscripts before me were an anthology, a succession of fragments, an archive more than a book," he recalled in an interview just after *Juneteenth*'s publication. Faced with this fragmentation, Callahan made the editorial judgment to publish one of those fragments, drawn from Ellison's most fully conceived section, Book II. To Callahan, it was Ellison's "most powerful, moving, compelling, and fully crafted material—the narrative where he is truly in his prime—was all but complete, an all but complete narrative within the whole."[6]

Three Days Before the Shooting . . . , which places *Juneteenth* in its larger textual context, at once bears out Callahan's judgment and complicates its implications. Clearly the material that constitutes Book II is superior stylistically to the rough-hewn episodic drafts Ellison assembled in the years before and the equally unperfected sequences he produced on the computer in the years that followed. Even in their imperfection, however, they reveal a far grander vision of Ellison's manuscript in progress than does *Juneteenth* alone.

"What he did was to leave fragments—some extremely fragmentary and others all but complete—of several potential novels or narratives within his saga," Callahan asserts in clarifying *Juneteenth*'s origins. Rather than constituting "several potential novels or narratives," it may be more useful to consider Ellison's narratives as distinct phases in the novel's composition. In other words, it is important to historicize the novel's composition, considering the disparate parts not as potential constituents of a single work but rather as Ellison's

evolving conception of the same material over time. This radically reorients our critical approach to the material, encouraging us to read what Ellison wrote not with an eye to com-
prising a novelistic whole but with a sense of imaginative
elasticity and historical contingency.[7]

Rather than reading the novel as a single text written over
forty years, an endeavor that ultimately has a leveling effect on
the material, elevating the inconsequential and relegating the
extraordinary to the same plan as the quotidian, it is essential
to conceive of the manuscript as a series of related but distinct
versions of the same novel written over time. In an essay entitled "The Making of Ralph Ellison's *Juneteenth*," Callahan
offers a useful three-part division of Ellison's long labor on the
second novel. He marks what he calls Ellison's "campaigns" to
compose a second novel as follows: an inaugural period spanning the book's earliest drafts in 1954 to the Plainfield fire in
1967; an intermediary period that begins right after the fire and
culminates in the 1972 typescripts that he revised once more in
early 1980s; and a final period that comprises all the material
Ellison would compose on the computer, beginning in 1982
and ending just a few months before his death in 1994. These
three periods are interrelated but distinct in the way they represent Ellison's concerted efforts to produce a publishable
manuscript. It is in the third phase, Ellison's work on the computer, where much of the mystery of the novel's incompletion
rests. Just as much as what he wrote, insight into the mystery
lies in how he wrote. As a third act in the story of his second
novel, this phase offers an insider's perspective into the fate of
fiction in the era of the personal computer.[8]

Ralph Ellison was a literary pioneer for the digital age. In composing his novel in progress on the computer he was among

the first authors enlisted, whether consciously or not, in a grand experiment measuring the effects of digital technology on the craft of fiction, an experiment that continues to this day. How does the computer affect the way writers write? How does it change their relation to language? What effect does it have on style and structure? The answers to these questions were largely unknown when Ellison began working on the computer. They are only marginally clearer today.

The computer has proved a mixed blessing at best for authors of creative fiction. As the center of gravity for a cultural revolution, computers have precipitated the rise of such casual and disposable forms of writing as e-mail, blogs, and, most recently, Twitter. They have also overseen the increasing marginalization of print media. The critic Kathleen Fitzpatrick has termed this sense of literature's impending demise the "anxiety of obsolescence." Such anxiety dominates much of the discussion when computers and novels collide. Still, literature maintains a crucial role in our culture, albeit one that will have to find its place in the world of new media, be it through e-books or other digital innovations. Similarly, digital technology will continue to shape how fiction is written. Many authors have found word processing to be an indispensable means of composition. But for those who remember an age before the personal computer, certainly for someone like Ellison, who was born just this side of the twentieth century, the freedoms such technologies promised came at a cost.[9]

Writing on the computer transformed Ellison's fiction—both its process and its product. It would be going too far to blame the computer for Ellison's failure to publish his second novel, but its impact on his writing was complicated and certainly not always positive. Writing fiction on the computer is a qualitatively different experience from writing by other means.

That which renders it liberating at first can ultimately lead to a stifling awareness of endless possibility. It is possible, in other words, for an artist to be too free. "The imagination wants its limits and delights in its limits," Nobel laureate Derek Walcott explains. "It finds its freedom in the definition of those limits." For a novelist of Ellison's particular cast of mind, one obsessed with transitions and the subtle modulations of syntax and diction, writing on the computer might have been the last kind of freedom he needed. This much is clear: if an answer can be found for why Ellison did not publish the book, a good part of it is locked up in his computer.[10]

The computer's complicity in Ellison's failure to produce his second novel is a painful irony. Computers, after all, are tools of efficiency; they have increased productivity in business and industry in ways unimaginable. Their effects on the arts have also been striking, if perhaps more equivocal. In the visual arts, digital technology has brought about tremendous advances in technique. In music, it has dramatically expanded the musician's soundscape while enabling listeners to amass huge audio libraries. In literature, it has made the great writings of the past accessible to a mass audience, often for the first time. It has transformed the way we approach reading, and certainly the way we approach writing.

For the novelist, the computer would seem an unmitigated boon. It obviates the time-consuming process of retyping multiple drafts. It liberates the mind to conceive new connections across the expanse of a fictive landscape. For some writers, the advent of the computer sparked a creative resurgence. The case of Henry Roth provides a compelling counterpoint to Ellison's experience. Like Ellison, Roth published an acclaimed novel early in his career then went decades without publishing a second. *Call It Sleep* (1934) announced the arrival of a promising literary talent. It had raw energy and narrative breadth, inspired in part by James Joyce. And yet it would be sixty years between Roth's published novels. In the last decades of his life Roth composed a massive six-volume work of fiction, four volumes of which have. been published (two posthumously) as a cycle entitled *Mercy of a Rude Stream*. He wrote the vast majority of this material on the computer; indeed, he casts the computer in the narrative itself as a kind of character. Critics have found much of Roth's late prose sterile when compared to the work of his youth, but none can discount the tremendous productivity he achieved so late in life.

Norman Podhoretz invokes Roth in "What Happened to Ralph Ellison," though the comparison, given Ellison's avid use of the computer, is even more apposite than Podhoretz could have known. "Late in life," he writes, "Roth found his tongue again (curiously through learning how to use a computer), and proceeded to pour forth what had been pent up for so many years into a very lengthy autobiographical novel (published serially in several volumes) that in my judgment was as wooden and amateurish as his youthful first novel had been alive and precociously accomplished." For Roth the computer worked like literary human growth hormone, extending his fictive capacity—if not his achievement—well beyond its years, albeit at a cost.[11]

Ellison's literary life after the computer shares something of Roth's tremendous productivity. Ellison, too, wrote thousands of pages. But his experience diverges from Roth's both in the obvious fact that Ellison would make none of this material available for publication and in that most of what he wrote on the computer constituted revisions of episodes conceived sometimes forty years earlier in typescript. Ellison's archive at the Library of Congress contains several boxes of episodic fragments, most of them typed on colored, undated sheets of paper that render in some fashion almost every scene he would work on in the last decade of his life. Ellison was forward thinking enough to adopt the computer yet atavistic in his preoccupation with these past literary conceptions. More baffling still for those who wished to see him publish the book, few of his efforts at revision attended to the fundamental textual challenges he had failed to solve in earlier phases of the novel's composition.

Ellison was grappling with problems of craft, with episodes and transitions and the decisions necessary to fashion from them a coherent novelistic whole. As he explained to Leon Forrest in 1972, "For me writing is re-writing. I sketch out an idea and it tends to grow. The image of blowing on a flame comes to mind here. The process of the novel has to do with the attempt to make an eloquent form, so that the sections are true." Nowhere is this more evident than in Ellison's computer files, where the sketch of an idea often grows to grand proportions without ever resolving itself. At times one wonders whether Ellison could have written the novel in perpetuity, fussing over diction, fiddling with transitions.[12]

It would be easy, then, to say with Jessica Winter, writing on Slate.com in 2008, that Ellison had become the consummate procrastinator. Indeed, it seems to be the case when one sees yet another cosmetic revision when a simple textual decision was required. But Ellison denies us even this certainty, complicating claims that his writing had somehow devolved in his later years into a sad redundant practice, typing the same thing over and over like Jack Nicholson's character in *The Shining*. Too much evidence of his creative vitality and purpose exists even in his last efforts at writing. For all of Ellison's obvious creative exertion, however, he seemed uninterested or unable to compose the handful of textual bridges that might have connected his disparate manuscripts in a cohesive narrative. The answer to this puzzle may lie less in the content of what he wrote or did not write and more in the way he went about writing in the first place.[13]

Those who knew Ellison best tend to describe his compositional style in one of two ways. Some, like Albert Murray, considered him a riffer, writing with a jazzman's attunement to form and inspiration, working the textual changes, playing by eye and by ear. Others, like R. W. B. Lewis, described him as a "knitter," conceiving episodes and then knitting them into a literary fabric. Both of these descriptions have their merits, and yet neither accounts for what Ellison seems to have done— and to have not done—as he labored on his novel on the computer. One certainly sees the riffer at work, improvising on discrete passages, even on individual words. But he often pulls back instead of playing through the changes. Of all the new riffs he composed, few if any served a functional role; instead, at their best they are beautiful arpeggios, flights of virtuosity with an intrinsic beauty but little more.

The knitter, too, is at work in Ellison, though the efforts are unfinished. If we analyze the dates on which Ellison saved particular files, we see a clear plan of revision. Between the spring of 1992 and the winter of 1993, Ellison revised and saved all but a handful of the files that comprise three narrative sequences. Ellison did not label these large portions of text, so in editing *Three Days Before the Shooting . . .* , John Callahan and I simply distinguished them by character and setting: "Hickman in Washington, D.C.," "Hickman in Georgia & Oklahoma," and "McIntyre at Jessie Rockmore's Townhouse." In July 1992 alone, Ellison saved new versions of every file in the "Hickman in Washington, D.C." sequence. And yet the final task, the one that would make his novel whole, remained undone. "It was a jolt realizing that what he left was not nearly finished," Callahan recalls. "There was not one coherent, continuous narrative. I suspect there never was." To understand why, it may help to look closely at Ellison's computer.[14]

Robert J. Sawyer is hailed as the "dean of Canadian science fiction," the recipient of the Hugo Award and the Nebula Award, and the author of such titles as *Terminal Experiment* and *Mindscan*. He writes the kind of fiction—and, it must be said, writes it very well—that Ellison wished to avoid when the disembodied voice intoned the opening lines of *Invisible Man* to him as he tried to write a prisoner-of-war novel. Nonetheless, Sawyer and Ellison share a common experience with writing fiction on the computer. Sawyer was born in 1960, the year Ellison published "And Hickman Arrives," the first excerpt from the second novel. By the time personal computers were readily accessible in the 1980s, Sawyer was a young man in his twenties while Ellison was nearing seventy. For all their obvious differences, these two authors shared a vital connection: they both favored—Sawyer still does—a word-processing program called WordStar.

To understand why such a seemingly inconsequential detail matters it is important to know something of how WordStar works. Unlike Microsoft Word or WordPerfect, the most common word-processing programs used today, WordStar functions entirely by keystrokes rather than drop-down menus and mice. It requires that its user employ these keystrokes to perform even the simplest operation. For those proficient in its method, it has the benefit of keeping the fingers in the touch-typing position at all times, facilitating the uninterrupted flow of expression. The program also employs a feature called "Merge Print," which allows users to string together a series of files to be printed through a typed command. There is evidence of Ellison's use (and occasional misuse) of this function throughout his computer files.[15]

All of this means that WordStar's interface is modeled on the longhand method of composition rather than on the typewriter. In an essay posted to his web site Sawyer explains the difference in detail:

> On a long-hand page, you can jump back and forth in your document with ease. You can put in bookmarks, either actual paper ones, or just fingers slipped into the middle of the manuscript stack. You can annotate the manuscript for yourself with comments like "Fix this!" or "Don't forget to check these facts" without there being any possibility of you missing them when you next work on the document. And you can mark a block, either by circling it with your pen, or by physically cutting it out, without necessarily having to do anything with it right away. The entire document is your workspace.
>
> On a typewritten page, on the other hand, you are forced to deal with the next sequential character. Your thoughts are focused serially on the typing of the document. If you're in the middle of a line halfway down page 7, your only easy option is to continue on that line. To go backwards to check something is difficult, to put in a comment that won't show when your document is read by somebody else is impossible, and so on. Typing is a top-

down, linear process, not at all conducive to the in-
tuitive, leaping-here-and-there kind of thought
human beings are good at.

One can see Ellison making full use of these freedoms in the
computer files. With the entire document as his workspace, he
had unfettered flexibility. This may have been the problem.
Certain authors respond favorably to the more proscriptive
demands of the typewriter. "Some writers," Sawyer explained
in an e-mail correspondence in 2005, "find the forced focus of
the typewriter to be useful in making them push ahead: you
have to get THIS NEXT WORD exactly right before you can serially go on to the following word, and, because revision is such
a pain, there's a tendency on the part of some writers to labor
harder to get a sentence right the first time on a typewriter: more
thinking before actually hitting the keys. Since a wandering
mind can be a bad thing for a writer, the loss of such focus that
comes with being able to easily fly around a document—type
a bit here; tweak a bit there—could potentially dumb-down
what the writer was producing." Many of the textual variants
seem to show Ellison absorbed in minutiae at the expense of
larger structural concerns. "Ellison sometimes tended to over-
elaborate and over-refine Hickman's language in the [com-
puter] versions and revisions, almost as if he was instructing
Hickman," Callahan explains, speaking of the crucial scene at
the Lincoln Memorial, rendered in the typescripts and in the
computer files. And yet the typewritten drafts exude a kind
of force and focus missing from the later versions. "Consciousness is, after all, by definition, the focusing of attention," Sawyer concludes, "the attending to a single thing to the exclusion
of all other possible things: typewriters force that, computers
don't." The fact that the computer became Ellison's means of

transacting a great deal of personal correspondence and business as well as the means of composing his novel might well have contributed to the lack of focus sometimes apparent in the drafts. Without a dedicated tool for composition—the pen and pad, the typewriter—Ellison may have suffered a psychological block.[16]

Speculating on the potential psychological inhibitions that may have precluded Ellison from finishing his work, however, is of limited use. The mystery persists. How could Ellison spend more than a decade almost exclusively on revisions and yet not finish the novel? Had he simply lost his nerve? It would be unfair to make this final period of the novel's composition bear all the weight of Ellison's failure to publish. After all, he spent nearly thirty years working on the book before he owned a computer. And yet certain fundamental changes in his compositional habits distinguish this last phase from all that came before. Through the 1950s and most of the 1960s Ellison conceived and developed his plot and characters. If we take him at his word, just before the Plainfield fire in 1967 the novel was nearing completion. His efforts in the 1970s, resulting in the Book I and II typescripts, seem to bear out this claim. These sequences would prove his most finished prose, perhaps the closest he would ever come to a publishable manuscript. Even as late as 1986, when he was already well into his computer revisions, he appears to have returned to these earlier typescripts to give them a final revision.[1] Why he did not publish them is unclear. In all of these phases of composition, Ellison seemed genuinely focused on revising his manuscript toward publication. Even as the years, the decades, passed by, his resolve seemed undaunted.[17]

In the decade during which Ellison revised his second novel on the computer he came no closer to resolving the fun-

damental compositional questions presented by the 1972 typescripts. For all the thousands of pages Ellison wrote in the last
decades of his life, he seems not to have written the compara-
bly few pages it likely would have taken to craft transitions between distinct narrative fragments. Rather than abandoning it
entirely for a new project or even envisioning new contexts
and characters for the present fiction, however, he seems curiously to have returned to the novel's earliest drafts, dating
from the mid-1950s through the 1960s. Largely abandoning the
well-honed Book I and II typescripts, he instead takes up the
raw material from the novel's infancy—the discarded drafts of
the novel from the 1950s and 1960s. The effects of this are striking, the contrast with the 1970s typescripts staggering. Such
radical reconstruction has tremendous implications for understanding Ellison's second novel; indeed, it forces us to reconsider any conclusions drawn solely from *Juneteenth*. As Book II
of the typescripts, *Juneteenth* stands in for the apex of Ellison's
achievement with the second novel in this crucial middle period of its composition. Those who have come to know Ellison's second novel by *Juneteenth* alone, however, are working
with an incomplete understanding of what Ellison produced.[18]

What Ellison recovers from the early years of the manuscript's composition are the makings of a novel that hardly re-
sembles the one promised by Books I and II. Oklahoma now
emerges as a coequal setting with Washington, D.C. Sunraider's assassination on the floor of the Senate, played to such
great effect in the prologue, is nowhere to be found. And Hickman, rendered at a distance through Ellison's third-person
narration, takes on an active voice through extended reveries
relayed in the first person. Most strikingly, the Washington,
D.C., section changes from the Faulknerian psychological fic-

tion of the typescripts to a picaresque fiction reminiscent of *Invisible Man*.

To read Ellison's computer drafts alongside the typescripts is to experience literary vertigo: we are at once familiar with characters and incidents but discombobulated by the method of their narration—the unfamiliar tone, pacing, and prose style that Ellison now employs. Books I and II are referenced only rarely in the numerous episodic drafts and notes Ellison saved to disk. With the significant exception of the scene in which McIntyre visits Jessie Rockmore's townhouse from Book I (the last scene, incidentally, Ellison would work on before his death), Ellison seems to have spent little time revising McIntyre's first-person narration. Although the computer files reprise much of the material from Book II, they do so in such a way that the material takes on an entirely new character. Action moves from the interior ruminations of Hickman and Sunraider to the exterior movements of Hickman and his parishioners. The seed of the plot in the typescripts—the assassination attempt on the Senate floor—is alluded to but overtaken by the incidental actions of Hickman touring familiar neighborhoods, visiting national monuments, even eating barbeque. Gone is the tensile sense of impending crisis, replaced by a ruminative quality reminiscent of an old man, nearing the end of his days, taking a backward glance at his life. Even the means of composition seems to have taken on this ruminative quality; rather than filling in the narrative gaps or working through tough textual challenges, Ellison refines and refashions scenes already revised numerous times earlier in drafts from the 1950s and 1960s and again throughout the 1970s and 1980s. Although Ellison seemed finally to pull together significant sequences in the 1990s, in these years he also troubled over single words and, as always, transitions. All the while a bold sense of aesthetic purpose captivated him: to write a novel that could somehow explain America to itself and to the world.

> So what's an American? Shucks, Hickman, It's all up for grabs! So sometimes it's us who're on target, sometimes it's others. And of ideal Americans there are only a few, and them mostly dead. As for us, we live in worlds within worlds, touching others cheek by jowl, and yet so far apart that when it comes to our ideals there's a "yes" in all our "no's," and a "no" in all our "yeses". . . . Black and white, we're all involved, but mainly [it's] the fault of folks who want to control everything and everybody but themselves.

Here Ellison muses on American identity through the voice of his protagonist, Alonzo Hickman, an old jazzman turned preacher. Reflecting on his days traveling the chitterling circuit, playing segregated dances in small Southern towns, enduring Jim Crow's petty indignities and occasional mortal threats, Hickman envisions the American character. His Americans are born of seeming oppositions: us and others, near and far, affirmation and dissent, black and white. He defines them mostly by what they are not: always on target, pliable to constraint, ideal human projections of moral principle. Americans, Hickman finally asserts, are a people distanced by difference yet implicated in a common national fate.

In Hickman's jazz-toned words Ellison offers a model for American citizenship—not simply for black Americans but for all. It should not surprise us that jazz, America's greatest contribution to world music, might provide a vocabulary for defining our national identity. Like America itself, jazz embodies both reality and possibility, familiar melody and improvisation. The jam session is a model for democracy in action, fusing many voices into one. "Jazz, like the country which gave it birth," Ellison wrote in his 1958 essay "The Charlie Christian Story," "is fecund in its inventiveness, swift and traumatic in its developments and terribly wasteful of its resources. It is an orgiastic art which demands great physical stamina of its practitioners, and many of its most talented creators die young." Embodying both the promise and the failure of American democracy, jazz has much to teach us about our national life. "Put it this way," Duke Ellington once wrote, "jazz is a good barometer of freedom... In its beginnings the USA spawned certain ideals of freedom and independence through which, eventually, jazz was evolved and the music is so free that many people say it is the only unhampered, unhindered expression of complete freedom yet produced in this country." Thelonious Monk, characteristically, was more concise than Ellington but no less emphatic. He was rumored to have once said this: "Jazz is freedom. Think about that. You think about that."[19]

Ellison conceived his second novel in terms of this fundamental connection between jazz and freedom. Indeed, the jam session would be the narrative structure he would adopt to achieve the broadest possible sense of human experience. It accounts for the episodic structure, the narrative discontinuity, that marks the manuscript. "If it were a jam session," he mused in an undated note, "all would start from single incident then proceed to give their own versions. This would allow for extremes of variation while based upon the basic themes, but the 'truth' would remain in the minds of Hickman and

Bliss (not Sunraider)." The incident, of course, would be the assassination attempt, and the versions would be McIntyre's, Hickman's, Sunraider's, and the range of secondary characters that are removed but still implicated in what occurs—Janey Glover, Love New, Cliofus, Leroy, Leewillie Minifees, Jessie Rockmore, Maud. Ellison intended each of these characters and their corresponding episodes, though at a seeming remove from the novel's central action, to build on the "basic themes" embodied in the novel's core narrative. The challenge, then, for the reader of Ellison's manuscripts is to read with an ear attuned to improvisational unities precisely because Ellison was unable to assemble them clearly for our eyes. The structures, however, are there for those willing to listen. Reflecting on the incidental nature of his fiction in another undated note, Ellison connected the "trivial chaos" with the central "disaster" of the assassination. "Rereading the Rockmore incident," he writes, "it appears that along with the car burning and the encounter with the senator's secretary et al, trivial chaos is building to some kind of disaster. Each complaint—LeeWillie's the crossedeyed woman's [Maud's], Rockmore's—are all concerned with serious matters that are not allowed to be viewed seriously." Ellison's concern for serious matters not allowed to be viewed seriously is a profound claim to the dignity and respect due to all citizens in a democracy.[20]

The most dramatic thing separating the second novel as imagined in the computer files from the second novel as rendered in the typescripts is the emergence of Hickman as hero and governing consciousness. His voice, freewheeling and funny, eloquent and at times blustering, comes to dominate Ellison's fiction in ways that likely even he did not expect. As early as 1959 Ellison mused to Albert Murray about Hickman "taking over the book," but it was nonetheless in dialectal relation to Bliss/Sunraider. Undoubtedly Book II includes rich reflections in Hickman's voice, and yet they almost always return to Bliss: the Juneteenth revival, the trip to the movie theater, Bliss's birth, even the shooting in which Hickman is almost an incidental presence to Sunraider's blustering, watching from the balcony.[21]

Hickman's emergence in the computer sequences, however, is accompanied by a reciprocal deemphasis of Bliss/Sunraider. As mentioned before, Ellison appears not to have rewritten the scene of the shooting, nor has he rendered "Cadillac Flambé," the rollicking episode in which a black man named LeeWillie Minifees burns his own Cadillac on the Senator's lawn. This is not to say that Sunraider is removed entirely from the plot; indeed, Hickman's purpose of reaching him to stave off the execution attempt is still the putative seed of the action. What has changed, it seems, is Ellison's interest or at least orientation to this central episode and its key character. Although he retains the shooting as the impetus for action, he extenuates in novelistic time the period between Hickman's arrival, "three days before the bewildering incident," and the incident itself. Like a jazzman holding a note through a measure, easing through the changes, he bends time to fit a new—or, rather, newly awakened—interest.

Whereas Book II covers the interceding three days (or two) between the prologue's account of Hickman's arrival and the shooting in seven pages, the computer sequence "Hickman in D.C." covers the same period in nearly 350—with more to follow: the computer sequence abruptly cuts off as Hickman and his deacon, Wilhite, are leaving Rockmore's townhouse, still two days before the assassination attempt. What is at stake in such a profound difference? Clearly such a change signals a radical transformation of intention on Ellison's part. Although the characters and many of the incidents remain the same, the novel has been transformed in startling ways. Both decisions rely on Ellison's conception of narrative temporality.

Ellison's decision to truncate time in the typescripts intensifies the reader's feeling: one gets the sensation of being wrapped up in incidents of moment. It has the effect of isolating and emphasizing Sunraider's mad speech from the Senate floor. It imbues the hospital scene that follows—something that would seem incapable of any narrative tension—with urgency. Hickman speaking to Sunraider as Sunraider goes in and out of consciousness, Hickman captured by memory and Sunraider caught up in feverish dreams, offer Ellison a rich temporal tableau. The past overlaps with the present in a continuous cycle of time. Hickman and Sunraider, Sunraider and his past self, Bliss, intertwine with one another in a thread of consciousness. The result is a narrative of often exquisite lyricism and profound depth, and yet one that can also leave one cold and distant. What made *Invisible Man* such a sensation, and what accounts for its enduring place in the canon, is that it ushers readers in with its first-person narration. Its broadly rendered characters are alive with tragicomic intensity. Its sense of exploration and adventure are reminiscent of Mark Twain's *Huck Finn*. And its narrator offers the haunting suggestion that "perhaps, on the lower frequencies, I speak for you." The typescripts of the second novel never admit as much. They inspire a certain reverence and appreciation rather than engagement and participation.

By contrast, the second novel as Ellison reimagined it in the computer files shares something of *Invisible Man*'s sense of freewheeling adventure. It is chockablock with incident. The period between Hickman's arrival in the nation's capital and the shooting, something Ellison gracefully gestures toward in a few pages, has become the subject of the narrative in Book II. By elaborating on the incidental, Ellison also amplifies Hickman's solitary voice, in isolation from Sunraider, who has yet to appear by the time the draft abruptly ends.

Rather than moving directly to the assassination attempt after Hickman and his parishioners arrive as in the typescript prologue, the computer sequence follows Hickman's group for the entire day. Dismissed by the Senator's secretary, Hickman and his followers are searched by security guards (the last scene that the computer sequence shares with Book II). After checking into the Hotel Longview, Hickman takes a nap, tries to intercept the Senator at his mistress's penthouse, attempts to contact the Senator through a "middle-of-the-road" newspaper, returns to the Senate offices but is turned back by a guard, looks for Walker Millsap (a notorious "white-folks watcher") only to be confronted by a vernacular character named Leroy who mistakes Hickman for "Chief Sam," notices a mural of Christ, returns to the hotel, where he daydreams in the lobby, talks with Deacon Wilhite, takes his parishioners sightseeing at the Lincoln Memorial, returns to the Longview to take a shower, retires to the lounge, where he studies a reproduction of Brueghel's *Landscape and the Fall of Icarus,* catches a cab with Wilhite to visit Aubrey McMillen at Jessie Rockmore's townhouse, and after encountering the wild scene within, leaves to return to the Longview, no closer to finding Sunraider than when the day began.

Ellison renders these episodes to great effect, drawing on what John Callahan termed the "riffer's muse" to fashion vignettes that, though often connected to one another only incidentally, prove quite satisfying in themselves. Hickman's extended riff on the *Fall of Icarus,* though provisionally tied through the backstory of the high-flying escape of Icarus and his father, Daedelus, to Ellison's theme of fathers and sons, finally comes across as a vehicle to display Hickman's virtuosity, his particular combination of provinciality (he is unfamiliar with the painting) and acuity (he grapples with the puzzle the image presents until he has mastered it). Indeed, most of these incidents, though they betray the vestiges of a connection to a novel about Hickman and Bliss, fathers and sons, are now repurposed to suit a new vision, one with Hickman as the focus.

Hickman has changed in the computer sequences, and with him, so has Ellison's novel. The computer files's most vivid encounters are at an almost unfathomable distance from Ellison's putative purpose of rendering Hickman's efforts to save the Senator. "Hickman in D.C." revels in the obsolescence of action, shifting the burden of meaning to Hickman's ruminations. At his most labored, Hickman takes on a quality more reminiscent of Ellison's essays than of the typescripts. At its most sublime, Hickman becomes as fully realized a character as Invisible Man. Unifying voice while complicating perspective, Ellison has made Hickman a richer and deeper character than in the typescripts, albeit at the cost of his antiphonal relationship with Bliss/Sunraider. Through Hickman, Ellison explores the contrasts and the connections in a bifurcated voice. He, Ellison writes, is of "two minds"—one doubtful, the other hopeful; one blues-toned, the other sanctified. A notable example of this duality comes during Hickman's solitary search through the streets of Washington when he encounters a mural depicting a black Christ's march to his crucifixion bearing a cross topped by a "bundle consisting of red, white, and blue cotton," partly unfurled. Hickman interprets this arresting religious and nationalist iconography in a way that a more limited character could not. Such a doubling of vision connects to a long-standing tradition in African-American expression balancing the faith of the spirituals with the tragicomic sensibility of jazz and the blues.

For Ellison only a jazzman, and particularly a jazzman turned preacher, could have captured the texture of voice and experience he wanted from Hickman. Writing in the introduction to *Shadow and Act* in May 1964, when the second novel was nearly a decade into its composition, Ellison articulated why jazz was so often the subject of his essays and why the jazz musician was almost a heroic figure in his imagination. The passage, in which he recollects his childhood emulation of the jazz musicians who would visit Oklahoma City and the ones, such as Charlie Christian and Jimmy Rushing, who would come of age there, is worth quoting for what it reveals about Hickman, the character who was even then taking over the novel:

> Looking back, one might say that the jazzmen, some of whom we idolized, were in their own way better examples for youth to follow than were most judges and ministers, legislators and governors. . . . For as we viewed these pillars of society from the confines of our segregated community we almost always saw crooks, clowns or hypocrites. Even the best were revealed by their attitudes toward us as lacking the respectable qualities to which they pretended and for which they were accepted outside by others, while despite the outlaw nature of their art, the jazzmen were less torn and damaged by the moral compromises and insincerities which have so sickened the life of the country.

Rather more amoral than immoral, these heroic figures promised to the young Ellison a life unrestricted by the social realities of segregation and racial animus. Inspired not only by the freedom embodied in jazz music but also by the liberated and sincere attitude of those who performed it, Ellison seems to have sought the same in his fiction through Hickman.[22]

Hickman's ruminations draw equally from both the sacred and profane sources of jazz music, referencing New Testament Scripture and black American folktales, the life of the spirit and the desires of the flesh. Hickman is such an effective vessel for Ellison's explorations of America because, despite— or is it because of?—his experiences in the profane world, he approaches life with wonder and openness. In some ways it could be argued that Hickman is even a more ambitious, if certainly less finished, character than Invisible Man. Where Invisible Man seems incapable of something like love—the nearest he comes is the comic scene with Sybil—Hickman is motivated by a love both filial (for Bliss/Sunraider) and romantic (for Janey, the estranged love of his youth). This capacity for love, and with it for loss, a signal deficiency of *Invisible Man,* is one of the least expected, but most powerful, contributions the second novel makes to Ellison's literary legacy.

In Alonzo Zuber Hickman, Ellison has fashioned a heroic American individual, alphabetically complete (A to Z), both "hick" and "man." Hickman embraces his own American identity and recognizes it in others as only someone who has seen it denied would do. In that way Hickman can be read as a fictionalized manifestation of Ellison's thinking on American life as reflected in his essays. Indeed, Hickman's voice takes on an almost essayistic quality in some of his long asides. This sometimes comes at a cost to the fiction.

In comparison to what Ellison had written in the past,

and in particular to what he had achieved with the 1970s type-scripts, Ellison's computer sequences seem like a failure. It would appear that Ellison is engaged in the Sisyphean task of recasting time and again the same limited number of scenes conceived decades before, sometimes down to the sentence. As far as bringing the novel to completion, the aim Ellison reiterated countless times in the last years of his life, the thousands of pages saved to disk are signs of either failure or forbearance: he simply could not figure out how to bring the material together, or perhaps he was patiently waiting for the right means, seeking it in the only way he knew how, by writing more and more words. To see Ellison struggling, parsing seemingly inconsequential details, deliberating over false choices, often undoing work already well done, is to witness the dissolution of his literary craft or, at the very least, the loss of his command.

There is a measure of poignancy in Ellison's continued revision of the same small group of scenes. As gestures to human fallibility, his efforts speak to a shared experience of struggle. For a novelist, particularly one as dedicated to craft as Ellison, this struggle also means possibility. John Updike observes that, as a general precept, "works written late in the writer's life retain a fascination. They exist, as do last words, where life edges into death, and perhaps have something uncanny to tell us." In Ellison's case, his last words, though inextricably linked to words he conceived decades before in the prime of his literary life, speak to the abiding purpose of Ellison's fiction and to his uncanny premonition of America's future as it approached the twenty-first century.[23]

Reading over these sequences, it is impossible to overlook the general decline in the quality of Ellison's prose. Ellison was nearing seventy when he purchased the computer and eighty when he did some of his most extensive work, so some diminution of skill might be expected. It seems, however, that an additional force is at work, something that points to fundamental challenges inherent in composing fiction on the computer. A common charge against the computer as a tool for fiction is that it is in essence a multifunctional device that distracts from the necessarily singular focus on composition. Ellison wrote letters on it, composed essays (including "An Extravagance of Laughter"), even conducted some of his personal business. Today, of course, this freedom is extended much more, with computers offering a wide array of distractions. We use the computer to play games, write e-mail, conduct real-time chats, surf the web, listen to music, talk to friends and family, watch television and movies.

Even without such distractions, Ellison faced the challenge of repurposing an instrument intended for business. Ellison's computer, after all, was called an "Executive." He was faced, in other words, with molding the computer to the specific use of the creative writer. In this regard, he shared an experience common to all writers in the digital age. Generations before, writers confronted a similar challenge with the advent of the typewriter, another instrument intended primarily for business. It is a testament to their success in harnessing the typewriter's capacity as a tool for creative expression that we most often think of typewriters in the nostalgic light of the hard-boiled writer cranking out pages by dim lamplight. This was a mastery achieved only over time, and with many casualties among those authors unable to adapt.[24]

Ellison's story, however, is not a tragic one of the writer unable to keep pace with the times, for he embraced the computer long before many other authors. Being in the vanguard, Ellison was among the first to face the challenge of being a "generative typist" on the computer—that is, not simply copying from some other source or taking dictation but, in fact, conceiving on the fly. Although Ellison appears to have done a fair share of writing with a printed draft at his side—be it an earlier typescript or a printout from his computer—he also composed a considerable amount directly on his machine. In this effort, he was assisted by WordStar, which was suited for the kind of generative work authors must do without breaking their flow.

Ellison knew better than anyone, however, the limitations of flow for the writer of fiction. Writing easily is not the same as writing well. "Well, I write sometimes with great facility," Ellison explained, decades before the advent of word processing, "but I question it; and I have a certain distrust of the easy flow of words and I have to put it aside and wait and see if it's really meaningful and if it holds up. It's an inefficient way of working, but it seems to be my way." Word processing provided an instrument that further facilitated the "easy flow of words" in ways Ellison could never have imagined in the 1960s. Just as the fluidity of Ellison's writing increased, so did his distrust of what he produced. This second-guessing is evidenced by the great number of variants with minor adjustments to style rather than substantive changes to incident.[25]

Flow, both its benefits and detriments, is at last the crucial factor in understanding what Ellison achieved on the computer, even as we are confronted with his signal failure to complete the manuscript. At its best, Ellison's second novel achieves a kind of lucidity, a force of eloquence unfamiliar even in the pages of *Invisible Man*. His greatest improvisations on the computer, particularly those departures that take him away from familiar fictional ground, are among the most captivating—if not always the most technically accomplished—pieces of writing Ellison produced.

The work Ellison did on the computer for the second novel is, of course, only part of the story of his manuscript in progress. The closest he appears to have come to completing some publishable version of the novel was actually a decade before, in the waning days of the civil rights movement, the era of Vietnam, and the aftermath of personal catastrophe, the 1967 fire at his and Fanny's vacation home in Plainfield, when he lost the only copy of a significant portion of the manuscript. It is to this conflicted period that we now turn.

II
1970

In 1970 Ralph Ellison was an author under siege. In the December edition of *Black World*, a special issue dedicated entirely to Ellison, Marxist critic Ernest Kaiser offered a withering assessment that captured the spirit of much of the criticism directed at Ellison at the time. "Ellison has become an Establishment writer," Kaiser wrote, "an Uncle Tom, an attacker of the sociological formulations of the Black freedom movement, a defender of the criminal Vietnam War of extermination against the Asian (and American Black) people, a denigrator of the great tradition of Black protest writing and, worst of all for himself as a creative artist, a writer of weak and ineffectual fiction and essays mostly about himself and how he became an artist. And ironically enough, Ellison has developed in this way and reached these conclusions at the very time when the Black people's liberation struggle has reached new heights."[1]

To Kaiser, Ellison was on the wrong side of almost every major question of the day affecting black Americans. Not only that, but he was a self-indulgent aesthete who cared little for the plight of his people. As another critic wrote in the same issue, "What may have been incisive in 1959 is cliché in 1970. What may have been an instructive allusion to white writers in the Sixties is Tomism in the Seventies." Such name-calling would seem below the level of discussion, and yet the spirit if not the substance of these critiques is revealing. As Jerry Gafio Watts notes, "Such attacks were significant precisely because they conveyed the attitudes of an Afro-American intellectual milieu in which Ellison often found himself entangled."[2]

Kaiser's denunciation was only the most outrageous example of the frequent criticism Ellison encountered during the 1970s, both in print and in person. Also appearing that December was James Alan McPherson's revealing portrait of Ellison, "Indivisible Man." McPherson described several instances of black college students heckling Ellison during campus visits. In a letter about Ellison written to McPherson, one young woman offered a more measured explanation of Ellison's unpopularity among her generation of black Americans, absent Kaiser's tone of spite. "Today's youth are angry, and many times this anger closes their ears to a different rationale," she explained. "Ellison's language and approach, I fear, attach to him the stigma of black bourgeois and conservatism. This figure does not communicate well with the vocal black youth." Described in these terms, the distance between Ellison and this new black audience seems like nothing more or less than a generational rift. Ellison's language was a particular mixture of black vernacular and Western high cultural sources. His approach, as always, was to think critically about black people's central place in American life. Although this message of democratic individualism and cultural hybridity was consonant with the goals of the civil rights era, it was at odds with the radicalized sensibility then gaining ascendancy.[3]

In 1968 the publication of *Black Fire*, edited by Amiri Baraka and Larry Neal, had sounded a new black declaration of literary independence. Capturing the spirit of the moment, the anthology included submissions from many of the major figures who would soon come to constitute the Black Arts Movement. They considered themselves making a necessary break from the past. Part of that past was Ralph Ellison. Writing in the afterword, Neal offered the following paragraph on Ellison; it reveals a great deal about Ellison's critical esteem at this crucial transitional moment in black art and politics.

> They [the writings and speeches of Franz Fanon and Malcolm X] are especially more pertinent than Ralph Ellison's novel, *Invisible Man*, which is a profound piece of writing but the kind of novel which, nonetheless, has little bearing on the world as the "New Breed" sees it. The things that concerned Ellison are interesting to read, but contemporary black youth feels another force in the world today. We know who we are, and we are not invisible, *at least not to each other.* We are not Kafkaesque creatures stumbling through a white light of confusion and absurdity. The light is black (now, get that!) as are most of the meaningful tendencies in the world.

Neal makes a sharp distinction between the "New Breed" of black writer, the "contemporary black youth," and the old guard of which Ellison is the prime example. Of course, this is part of a generational cycle; youth almost always fashion their identities in contradistinction to the past. But it is more than that. Neal is also arguing for the visibility of blacks to one another as the new standard of reference rather than the presumed standard Ellison posits of blacks to whites. Leaving aside that Neal fails to acknowledge that Ellison's Invisible Man is perfectly legible to the black characters in the novel—to the vet doctor, to Mary, to Brother Tarp, and even to Bledsoe—what Neal is communicating takes its force less as literary criticism than as cultural call to arms. Using Ellison's trope of invisibility as a cipher, he makes a radical claim for black visibility as a way of recentering his readers' point of reference.[4]

Neal's criticism of Ellison would be echoed and sharpened in the years to come by a host of black critics who imagined Ellison as a capitulator, assimilationist, and Uncle Tom. Interestingly, Neal would reconsider his critique of Ellison just two years later, calling for a more nuanced understanding of Ellison's writing and beliefs. In an act of intellectual bravery and integrity, he recanted his previous assessment of Ellison in the pages of *Black World*. But Neal was an exception among Ellison's critics. Many held to their criticisms and character assassinations of Ellison to the end.

For his part, Ellison did the best he could to seem above the fray. Speaking to Robert Penn Warren, Ellison addressed charges of Tomism. "I've never pretended for one minute that the injustices and limitations of Negro life did not exist," he said, measuring his words. "On the other hand I think it important to recognize that Negroes have achieved a very rich humanity despite these restrictive conditions. I wish to be free not to be less Negro American but so that I can make the term mean something even richer. Now, if I can't recognize this, or if recognizing this makes me an Uncle Tom, then heaven help us all."[5]

Ellison's many appeals to American identity and to the complex hope for multiracial democracy came across as traitorous to a younger generation of black Americans feasting on the rhetoric of separatism and suffering from integrationist fatigue. Emerging out of the cultural and political flux of the late 1960s was a younger generation inspired by the clenched militancy of the Black Panther Party and the Black Arts Movement. They looked askance at what they saw as Ellison's capitulatory politics and elitist aesthetics. With the Vietnam War continuing its downward spiral into chaos and the increasing atmosphere of protest at home, with the fomenting racial tensions between black and white emerging out of America's urban centers and a cultural war under way along generational lines, Ellison seemed like a man out of phase with his time.

Despite Kaiser and other critics' claims to the contrary, Ellison was certainly in touch with the discourses of the post–civil rights era. Although his critics painted Ellison's opinions as quaint or even dangerously backward, his concern for America's multiracial future would endure even as the popularity of black nationalism diminished. Indeed, some of those who rejected Ellison in the late 1960s and early 1970s would return to him by the middle of the decade. Throughout this ordeal Ellison offered few public responses to his detractors, though he expressed considerable anger and frustration in private at what he perceived to be profound mischaracterizations of his belief and mismeasure of his motives. It was in his writing, and particularly in his work on the second novel during this critical period between the 1967 fire and the completed revision of the typescripts in 1972, that Ellison offers his most emphatic response—not simply to his critics but to the challenge of achieving black equality in a new era of freedom.

Even as Ellison was experiencing popular disaffection, he was finding his creative inspiration reborn. Finally seeming to have recovered from the fire that had destroyed a summer's worth of work on his second novel, he published two excerpts in two years: 1969's "Night-Talk" in the *Quarterly Review of Literature* and 1970's "A Song of Innocence" in the *Iowa Review*. These publications are remarkable given that he had previously published only four other excerpts; together they suggest that Ellison was not simply reconstructing but actually reenvisioning his novel so long in progress. By the summer of 1972 he had completed revisions on the typescripts to Books I and II, and once again was talking about publishing the novel.

When Richard M. Nixon took the oath of office on January 20, 1969, the civil rights movement effectively ended. His predecessor, Lyndon B. Johnson, had helped usher in the great legal advances in the equality of black Americans as a part of his Great Society program. Even as Johnson's escalation of the war in Vietnam lead America into a morass abroad, his leadership on issues of race helped the nation weather tumultuous political struggles at home. In his famous commencement address delivered at Howard University on June 4, 1965, Johnson laid out an ambitious set of national goals: "To shatter forever not only the barriers of law and public practice, but the walls which bound the condition of many by the color of his skin. To dissolve, as best we can, the antique enmities of the heart which diminish the holder, divide the great democracy, and do wrong—great wrong—to the children of God."[6]

In sharp contrast, Nixon counseled slowing, if not halting, the advance of desegregation and equal rights. In his 1970 State of the Union address he cautioned that "it is time for those who make massive demands on society to make some minimal demands on themselves." Such a thinly veiled critique of supposed black dependency overlooked the massive efforts that black Americans were already making to better their own stake while overlooking the endemic oppression at work in American society. Shortly thereafter, a startling memo to Nixon from a key domestic adviser, Daniel Patrick Moynihan, was leaked to the press. In it Moynihan advised Nixon to pursue a policy of "benign neglect" on issues of race. The memo was greeted by outrage from black leaders and their liberal white supporters, but it is worth revisiting the memo for the light it sheds on this pivotal period of historical transition.

> The time may have come when the issue of race could benefit from a period of "benign neglect." The subject has been too much talked about. The forum has been too much taken over to hysterics, paranoids, and boodlers on all sides. We may need a period in which Negro progress continues and racial rhetoric fades. The Administration can help bring this about by paying close attention to such progress—as we are doing—while seeking to avoid situations in which extremists of either race are given opportunities for martyrdom, heroics, histrionics, or whatever. Greater attention to Indians, Mexican-Americans and Puerto Ricans would be useful. A tendency to ignore provocations from groups such as the Black Panthers might also be useful. (The Panthers were apparently almost defunct until the Chicago police raided one of their headquarters and transformed them into culture heroes for the white—and black—middle class. You perhaps did not note on the society page of yesterday's *Times* that Mrs. Leonard Bernstein gave a cocktail party on Wednesday to raise money for the Panthers. Mrs. W. Vincent Astor was among the

> guests. Mrs. Peter Duchin, "the rich blonde wife of
> the orchestra leader," was thrilled. "I've never met a
> Panther," she said. "This is a first for me."

Moynihan's words were simply characterized as racist by many
when they were, in fact, something more complicated than
that. He was right to suggest that rhetoric had largely overtaken action among some of the most prominent voices of
black leadership by 1970. The pernicious element of the memo,
rather, is the moral exhaustion it expresses in relation specifically to the cause of black rights. Moynihan even goes so far
as to target other minority groups for attention, not as part of
an overall strategy for racial equality, but at the expense of a
black minority that had, in Nixon's words, made "massive demands upon society." Moynihan, who had established a repu-
tation as a scholar on race and ethnicity with such volumes as
Beyond the Melting Pot (published in 1963 with Nathan Glazer)
and *The Negro Family: The Case for National Action* (1965),
seemed to confirm with his memo the very conspiracy theories
that sustained groups on the fringes of the social contract. His
reference to "martyrdom, heroics, histrionics or whatever"
seemed to dismiss the blood sacrifice of those leaders who had
fought for nothing more than equal justice.[7]

The dangerous fallacy at work in Moynihan's memo, and
equally at work in the rationale of many of his critics, is that
black equality comes at the discretion of whites alone. Although it was undoubtedly whites—and specifically, white
men—who had to hand down the Supreme Court rulings and
vote on the congressional legislation that ensured the equality
of all Americans under the law, the true struggle for equality
was far more complicated, and far more collaborative, than

that. Even a decade before the passage of the Civil Rights Act
of 1964 and the Voting Rights Act of 1965, Ellison had written
to his friend Morteza Sprague soon after the *Brown v. Board*
decision, "Well so now the Court found in our favor and recognized our human psychological complexity and citizenship
and another battle of the Civil War has been won. The rest is
up to us and I'm very glad."[8] Ellison was suggesting not that
the government no longer had a responsibility to protect the
rights of all its citizens but rather that black Americans were—
and had to be—active participants in their freedom. Ellison believed that black freedom, like American freedom more
generally, required a national commitment to realizing our
vaunted principles in the practice of governance.

The problem with "benign neglect" and the laissez-faire
spirit of racial politics that it supported is that it forestalled essential conversations across the racial divide. Discussions on
race—and particularly discussions of black Americans' place
in a newly integrated de jure reality, and a defiantly segregated
de facto one—ended precisely when they needed to begin.
This was not the sole result of a single memo or presidential
administration. Numerous factors contributed to the silence.
The Vietnam War had escalated, as had protests at home. The
assassinations of the 1960s robbed the nation of some of its
finest leaders, culminating in the deaths of Martin Luther
King, Jr., and Robert Kennedy within months of each other.
Urban race riots exploded in America's major cities, stimulat-
ing fear in a white public that might otherwise have been positively disposed to racial equality. The Black Panther Party and
other advocates of black power politics sometimes foreclosed
transracial discussion in the name of what many young blacks
felt was a necessary militancy. White moral exhaustion set in,

particularly at a time of economic struggle for all. And, yes, the Moynihan memo signaled a betrayal of Lyndon Johnson's Great Society, which, flawed as it was, at least promised to keep at the center of the nation's attention the issue of blacks entering the public sphere as equal citizens.

All of these developments conspired to foreclose the essential discussions and *actions* the nation needed to undertake after expanding the civic culture by such artificial and traumatic means. The Civil War had its Reconstruction, and though it was soon betrayed by the Hayes-Tilden Compromise of 1877, it demonstrated the difficulty, but also the necessary commitment, it would take to ensure that America lived up to its promise as a multiracial democracy. Such a dramatic remodeling of the nation does not happen as we sleep.

And yet by 1970 an uneasy hibernation had settled over the issue of racial justice. After more than a year in office, Nixon had not directly addressed civil rights and had only begrudgingly entered into the debate over implementing school desegregation. Meanwhile, the dominant black political voice had shifted from the civil rights leadership's appeal to American principles to an outright rejection of those principles in favor of a new black isolationism, wishing to remove itself from the corrupting influence of white America. The optimism of the movement wavered in the face of the impending realities of life on the night side of American prosperity. For Ellison, the answer to this challenge lay not simply in white benevolence but also in the knowledge that black Americans had gained through the very experience of white supremacy. "The rest," as he had written to Morteza Sprague, was "up to us." In 1970 this would prove a difficult argument for many to accept. Ellison was about to offer his own response to the present day realities of post–civil rights America, his alternative to racial fatigue and his rejoinder to what he called "the blackless fantasy."

On March 10, 1970, Ralph Waldo Ellison received a letter addressed to him as "Ralph G. Ellison" from the senior editor of *Time*, John T. Elson, detailing a proposed article to be included in a special issue on blacks in America. "We have in mind," Elson wrote, "an article of between 2,000 and 2,500 words that addresses itself, as you see fit; to two hypothetical questions: what would America have been with the blacks? What would it be like today without them?" Elson's questions presented curiously conflicting propositions—the first presuming black absence from American history, the second asserting a problematic presence. From little more than this scant suggestion, Ellison would write a kind of manifesto, articulating in clear terms his fundamental beliefs about the essential importance of black Americans to the nation's culture and democracy.[9]

"What America Would Be Like without Blacks" is among Ellison's best-known essays. It first appeared in *Time* on April 6, 1970, and would be reprinted in 1986 in *Going to the Territory*, Ellison's second collection of essays. Yet the details of its genesis are as remarkable as they are obscure. Perhaps most surprising is that Ellison seems to have written the piece in no more than a week. Between *Time*'s March 10 letter soliciting the essay and its March 19 letter offering final editorial changes, Ellison conceived and composed this striking statement of belief. Originally titled "The Blackless Fantasy," the essay is one of Ellison's most strenuous arguments for the centrality of blacks to the American experience. It is punctuated by Ellison's memorable claim that "whatever else the true American is, he is also somehow black." Reading through Ellison's multiple drafts and his correspondence with the editors of *Time,* however, adds texture to this message. It reveals Ellison's essay not simply as a strong assertion of principle but also as only the most visible part in process that began before and would continue after the essay's publication. This broader context imbues Ellison's essay with a certain historicity, revealing it as a product of this particularly turbulent moment in Ellison's life and the history of the nation.

Reading *Time*'s letter of March 10, the editors' vision of the essay Ellison would write is clear. Elson even includes notes on "our feeling" on the topic. It is striking to read these suggestions next to what Ellison produced. "Perhaps the argument could be made," Elson begins, "that the presence of the black in a predominantly white society—the presence of an enslaved people belatedly raised to freedom—has forced America to wrestle with its conscience, and to face up to the ugly underside of human character." Ellison, of course, refuses to subject blacks to the passive role of social barometer, instead insisting on their active role not simply in securing their own freedom but in defining the meaning of freedom for all Americans. Blacks, in other words, move from object to subject. Rather than focusing, as the editors suggest, on the "ugly underside of the human character," Ellison renders the more complex and confounding above-side of hope and struggle for freedom. Ellison's essay rejects such pessimism in favor of a view of American life that, though not quite optimistic, is at least hopeful of its potential.[10]

Time's editors next try to wax poetic on black "contribution" to America: "Without the contribution of the blacks—their particular wisdom, their experience of agony and tragedy, their humor, and so on—white America would be a monochromatic nation, a larger and wealthier version of Canada, perhaps, or a Sweden without the midnight sun." This passage suggests a couple of things: first that the editors should leave the writing to writers, and second that *Time* is all but ignoring the multiracial reality then emerging in the United States. This biracial sensibility hearkens back to old ways of race thinking, swiftly changing in the twentieth century. "We offer you these thoughts not to limit your essay but simply to indicate how we at TIME have initially framed the questions in our minds."[11]

Ellison's essay is written against the backdrop of a tumultuous era in American race relations, one in which the dominant ideology of black separatism and nationalism emerged. Ellison makes only passing references to contemporary events (he mentions Moynihan's memo, and references to Flip Wilson and Spiro Agnew were excised from the published essay), but his essay is undoubtedly a response to black nationalists. Filtering through the past, Ellison approaches the present crisis in an historical context that allows him to cast the present as part of the continuing challenge of perfecting American democracy. Instead of calling black nationalism by name, he refers to it as "neo-Garveyism," no doubt as a means of discrediting it but also as a way of articulating its proper lineage. Ellison presents himself as the mediating voice between two extremes that, ironically, have worked toward the same goal: the extrication of blacks from the nation. Ellison begins the essay by identifying the "tragic themes of American history" that have reawakened in the present moment. They include white Americans' "moral fatigue" in relation to black Americans' desire for equality, black Americans' "ceaseless (and swiftly accelerating) struggle to escape the misconceptions of whites," and the conflation of race with culture when blacks are concerned. All of these are embodied, Ellison argues, in the fantasy of extricating the black presence from America—either by expulsion or by secession.[12]

The fantasy of a blackless America, Ellison argues, "becomes operative whenever the nation grows weary of the struggle toward the ideal of American democratic equality." What both expulsionists and secessionists share is a common belief in the efficacy of such mobility, that blacks can readily remove themselves—or be removed—from the American context. Although this has often been theorized, and even occasionally been attempted, it has never been successful. The reason, Ellison posits, has as much to do with culture as with politics. On the level of culture, the melting pot has already melted, "creating such deceptive metamorphoses and blending of identities, values and life-styles that most American whites are culturally part Negro American without even realizing it." Several paragraphs later he picks up this thread again. "Despite his racial difference and social status, something indisputably American about Negroes not only raised doubts about the white man's value system, but aroused the troubling suspicion that whatever else the true American is, he is also somehow black." What makes this revelation so troubling is the dogged insistence on enforcing the boundaries of racial exclusion.[13]

Ellison articulates broad claims for black agency, ones that extend well beyond the boundaries of skin color. Ellison's America can only be understood as a product of the black experience, just as it is also indebted to Western European inheritances. At a time when black power was the word, it is hard to imagine ascribing more power to the blackness than Ellison does here, endowing black Americans with the capacity to shape a nation. "Materially, psychologically and culturally, part of the nation's heritage is Negro American," he writes, "and whatever it becomes will be shaped in part by the Negro's presence." He continues,

> Which is fortunate, for today it is the black American who puts pressure upon the nation to live up to

its ideals. It is he who gives creative tension to our struggle for justice and for the elimination of those factors, social and psychological, which make for slums and shaky suburban communities. It is he who insists that we purify the American language by demanding that there be a closer correlation between the meaning of words and reality, between ideal and conduct, between our assertions and our actions. Without the black American, something irrepressibly hopeful and creative would go out of the American spirit, and the nation might well succumb to the moral slobbism that has always threatened its existence from within.

Black Americans, in other words, represent a national hope. They embody the essence of American identity precisely because they challenge the limits of freedom. "They are an American people who are geared to what *is*, and who yet are driven by a sense of what it is possible for human life to be in this society," he continues, moving toward conclusion. "The nation could not survive being deprived of their presence because, by the irony implicit in the dynamics of American democracy, they symbolize both its most stringent testing and the possibility of its greatest human freedom."[14]

With such a striking tone of hope, it comes as a surprise that anyone could read within it anything as limited as racism. Yet that is precisely what happened. Among Ellison's files relating to "What America Would Be Like without Blacks" is a two-page letter from one S. D. Claghorn of Orange, California, dated May 2, 1970. "You are a black bigot—I am a white bigot," Claghorn writes. "Your adherence to black racism is opposed to my white racism but the confounding difference is that my basis for superiority has validity." What follows is a racist screed in which Claghorn rails against the "pure hell your people have raised in this country" and the threat of miscegenation. "You will not agree to anything in the foregoing," he concludes, "even as I do not agree with you, so we are going to an explosive collision. When we have cleaned our political houses of the fawning misfits who are supposedly representing us, there must and will be, changes." He then concludes, rather opaquely, "Black is not beautiful—if you don't like black."[15]

The most striking thing about Claghorn's letter is not its content but rather Ellison's response.

> Dear Mr. Claghorn:
>
> Thank you for your letter of May 2, written in criticism of my essay which I was invited to write for the April 6th issue of TIME magazine.
>
> My response is simple: I am quite willing to admit that I am inferior if you are willing to admit that I wrote *Invisible Man*. Sincerely yours,"

Ellison never signed or mailed the letter; it is marked "unsent" in Ellison's hand. But it offers a glimpse at Ellison's anger, here taking the shape of a glib brashness. Ellison seems to be saying that he, himself, offers the very proof of his case: black achievement in culture is the greatest defense.[16]

The hopeful notes of coexistence and connection that Ellison had struck in "What America Would Be Like without Blacks" belied the dominant tone of peril that seemed to accompany many discussions of race relations in 1970. In the very issue of *Time* in which Ellison's essay appeared, most of the other articles portrayed a black population in no mood to embrace their American identity. The cover story featured a young Jesse Jackson bloviating on what blacks are going to do for themselves and what they are "going to make the Man do." Other articles featured the Black Panther Bobby Seale in conversation with more moderate leaders like Julian Bond and Whitney Young, Jr. Throughout, the articles pressed the concept of "Two Americas," emphasizing black militancy and struggle in "the White Man's World." An introductory essay begins with a quotation from Malcolm X and this startling line: "The struggle between the races in America is indeed the struggle for the soul of a nation." "More than a century after the Civil War and 16 years after the Supreme Court's school-desegregation ruling," it continues, "the American black has not achieved justice or equality. This remains the biggest single problem in America, and its greatest shame. Unless the problem is solved, all of U.S. urban civilization may dissolve in a mixture of chaos and repression." For a magazine intended for a middle-American white audience, this was strong language. It speaks to the level of saturation the racial crisis had reached by 1970.[17]

The most obvious sign of impending chaos was the continued spread of civil disturbances, primarily in America's urban centers. Between 1964 and 1971 as many as seven hundred race-related riots erupted in the United States. Some were in response to particular events, like the assassination of Martin Luther King, Jr., in April 1968; others were the product of continued socioeconomic inequality and pent-up frustration that the victories of the civil rights movement seemed not to have had a real effect on the lives of many of the poorest blacks. Such tangible expressions of frustration fed into the more philosophical ones that led many young blacks to demand such clenched militancy even from their literature. A month after his *Time* essay, Ellison's name appeared again in a brief review published in *Life* entitled "Native Son Strikes Home" by

Clifford Mason, a young black playwright of modest renown.
Mason recast Irving Howe's earlier comparison of Ellison to
Richard Wright, but this time arguing not only for Wright's superior claim to black authenticity but to his greater political
relevance in a time of national turmoil. "The problem of Bigger Thomas is the problem of our times," he wrote. "The cities
are burning, almost as if inspired by Wright's three-decade old
prophesy." He ended the article with a quotation from Bigger's
lawyer, Max, prophesying the murderous rage building up in
"a wild cataract of emotion that will brook no control."[18]

Reading Mason's two-column story with the lengthy
Ellison-Howe exchange from a few years earlier in mind points
up striking differences. Whereas Howe's argument had the
virtue of a certain critical nuance, Mason's is baldly propagan-
distic, taking every opportunity to assassinate Ellison's character. Mason offers the acclaim *Invisible Man* received from
white critics as proof positive of Ellison's racial treachery. "Part
of the reason for such grandiloquent praise," Mason conjec-
tures, "lay in their strong reaction to the obsequious bleatings
of white appeasement that have characterized Ellison's politics." Rather than supporting this charge, he immediately turns
back to Wright, as if such imprecations against Ellison were
proof in themselves. The remainder of the piece consists of a
series of invidious comparisons whereby Mason judges Wright
superior to Ellison in every category—from literary style (*Invisible Man* is marred by its "overextended 'postimpressionist'
flow," whereas *Native Son* demonstrates a "tightly controlled
plot line"), to politics (Ellison's novel is deeply indebted to the
Communist Party, whereas Wright's is only incidentally so), to
character development (Bigger Thomas's struggle is a powerful study in character, whereas Invisible Man's invisibility is
finally "merely vacuous"). He offers these comparisons in the

name of "rectifying the great disservice white critics have done to all black literature over the years by praising Ellison at the expense of Wright." Mason would extend this case against Ellison a few months later in a longer piece in the aforementioned special issue of *Black World*.

Something more was at stake, however, in the renewal of this familiar comparison between Wright and Ellison than had been in previous instances. Wright, dead since 1960, no longer presented the inconvenience of a living author, filled with contradictions and opinions. Ellison, in contrast, though of a older generation, was very much active, representing many of the perspectives that had put him in disfavor among the Marxists in the 1930s, won him praise in the civil rights era, and now again found him out of favor with a younger generation entranced by black power politics. Ellison, in other words, was an easy mark for those attempting to enforce a new racial orthodoxy that brooked no divergence. Reading Ellison's writing in 1970, one gets the sense of a writer continuing to develop his favored themes, extending them both in fiction and in nonfiction. What one does not see, however, is a writer responding to the numerous attacks against his character. Indeed, one could get the sense that he had bunkered himself in. But this would be far from the truth.

Less than two weeks after Mason's *Life* article appeared, Ellison sent a letter to his attorney to be forwarded to the editors of *Life*. In eleven typed pages, he fashions a remarkable document that offers a rare glimpse into the private turmoil these public criticisms inspired. Part rhetorical parry, part literary essay, Ellison's unpublished letter is a defiant articulation of his core beliefs that is so disproportionately powerful when compared to Mason's piece that it might better be read as Ellison's response to the era itself. Ellison begins by calling atten-

tion to the "mounting turmoil of racial antagonism that is
helping to tear our country apart," of which Mason's article is
but one small example. After rebutting Mason's particular
charges against him and offering a rich account of his relationship to Richard Wright, he reaches a pitch of eloquence
on the ninth page. It begins, humbly enough, with a curt dis-
missal of Mason. "All living things are critics, it has been said,"
he writes, "and LIFE has affirmed that it believes this critic
[Mason] alive by welcoming him to its pages. But that, I'm
afraid, is about all it has affirmed." Rather than pursue this line
of critique further, something that would have undoubtedly
smacked of bullying, he instead opens up his analysis to the
very spirit of racial and intellectual parochialism of which
Mason is but a minor example. The passage is worth quoting
at length.

> For there is a smell about this enterprise, an odor
> rank of enclosed rooms of the mind, a stench re-
> vealing a fear to face up intellectually to the com-
> plications of literature no less than to those of a
> multi-racial, pluralistic society. It is a fear that
> would reduce important conflicts of vision to petty
> motives and all complexities of culture and person-
> ality to the rank over-simplifications of racial hos-
> tility. Never in this view could a black American be
> judged worthy of recognition as a leading *American*
> writer, for to do so demands a mind open to the
> possibilities which exist within this racist society
> *despite* its racism and its perplexing contradictions
> of caste and class. Being an American, Henry James
> has written, is a complex fate; and being a black

American is more complex than even that finely
honed mind could ever have suspected. Because for
blacks freedom is always hedged with traps and
contradictions, and one of the saddest aspects of
being a black American who strives for freedom of
expression is that one's assertion of freedom often
frightens one's fellow blacks far more than it frightens even the most bigoted whites.

This is a credo for Ellison's political aesthetics—conscious of
racism, but mindful of possibility; cognizant of difference,
but alive to interplay of racial categories. Like every black
writer since the slave narrators, and like so many others
throughout the American tradition, Ellison embraces freedom as the dominant force behind artistic creation. He articulates a frightening freedom for black Americans, one that
confronts the complexities of a "multi-racial, pluralistic society" without the easy defense of racial chauvinism. Ellison understood this as the challenge of the post–civil rights generation, the inevitable next step after securing legal rights. The
freedom Ellison defines is a matter both of personal belief and
of national calling; it is freedom of expression and of democratic virtue.[19]

To say that Ellison portrays himself as a martyr in this
letter may be going too far, and yet there is something within
it that sounds of reluctant resignation to judgment coupled
with unwavering faith in the rightness of his cause. Ellison
comes across by turns as stubborn, defensive, enraged, and
amused but, more than anything else, as committed to
a common set of national principles. Here again, as he had
in his *Time* essay, Ellison insists that "American" is broad

enough to encompass black Americans without effacing racial identity.

To many among the younger generation of black Americans, Ellison's calls to collective identity smacked of capitulation. One of the most unseemly stories to emerge from Ellison's life in this era has him breaking down in tears on the shoulder of a bewildered college student after suffering the outburst of another student calling him an Uncle Tom. Arnold Rampersad relates the 1967 incident in his biography of Ellison, telling of Ellison's tearful insistence to the consoling student, "I'm not a Tom, I'm not a Tom." For an individual known for his self-possession in public, such evidence of hurt and vulnerability is almost unthinkable. It connects to the private history of Ellison's relation to his own public image, recounted in the personal letters and unpublished responses to those who would question his racial allegiance.[20]

Ellison approaches his critics not through the language of personal attack but through the terms of social experience. Yet again we see him asserting his faith in the unpredictable and undeterred expression of black life. Unstated in all of this is the fundamental tension that many younger blacks identified in Ellison's beliefs between race consciousness and cosmopolitanism, between being a race man and an American patriot. At base, Ellison proposes a broader sense of freedom to define blackness. As he explained plainly in an undated note, "I have very low regard for Negro Americans who've allowed themselves to identify as (to reduce themselves to) 'blacks' under the pressure of Anglo-Euro-Americans who have allowed chosen to (reduce themselves to) identify themselves as 'whites.'" Those who follow this path, he argues, have "been so foolish as to assume that because white was powerful economically and politically, this also gave them cultural identity *and* superiority." Ellison saved equal scorn for what he saw as the oversimplifications of black power politics and black-is-beautiful aesthetics, both of which he believed ironically housed an implicit assertion of white superiority. "Both are false," he argued. "*Some* blacks are beautiful and many are not. Some whites are superior (as are some blacks) but most are not. Some black are creative. Some whites are creative. Most are not but that leaves much to be said of human value." Behind Ellison's rejection of all racialism is his profound faith in a shared American identity. This is not simply a matter of principled idealism but of pragmatic practice: Ellison knew that blacks were ill-equipped to win in the game of racial one-upmanship; our hope, the hope for the nation, was to locate our shared humanity in the specific terms of our national identity.[21]

Ellison's public branding as an apologist for the status quo can be embodied in a single incident: his refusal to stand with other artists in boycotting the 1965 White House Arts Festival to protest the Johnson administration's actions in Vietnam. Leading the protest was the poet Robert Lowell. Ellison, who attended the event, later commented on the Lowell-led protest: "I think this was unfortunate. The President wasn't telling Lowell how to write poetry, and I don't think he's in any position to tell the President how to run the government." He went on to draw a comparison to his experiences in the 1930s Left. "I was very much amazed, having gone through the political madness that marked the intellectual experience of the 'thirties,' to see so many of our leading American intellectuals, poets, novelists—free creative minds—once again running in a herd." Jerry Gafio Watts makes much of this instance in arguing for Ellison's "antiliberal conception of democracy" and

vision of the ideal author as "politically disengaged." Certainly
Ellison's response to the protest and, more generally, to all
public protests, is one of disengagement, yet his overall relation to political action is something more expansive and complicated. Ellison's notes, personal correspondence, and above
all, his fiction testify to his keen political awareness, driven by
a vision of responsible citizenship and civic action. In a revealing note found among Ellison's papers he writes the following:
"There is now being exhibited some of the same sentimental-
ity concerning the war in Viet Nam which white Americans
showed toward the South after the Civil War. . . . Only more so
because it is so easy and cheap. Indeed, many of the poets and
intellectuals who lead this hysteria identified with the South
and had absolutely no sympathy for the slaves or their descendents. I find this disgusting." Ellison perceived a disconnect between the principled stance on foreign affairs and the absence
of principle in the domestic arena. This private note, charged
as it is with unmistakable and clearly directed anger, offers a
more nuanced perspective on his public dispute with Lowell
and the other artists and intellectuals who supported the
White House boycott. Ellison's difference was not simply one
of style or of decorum—a respect for the office of the presi-
dency or a knowledge of one's "place" in the political realm—
but of a substantive difference of politics and principle. His
call for consistency is a challenge to his fellow artists to take
more than symbolic action, to act with similar conviction in
their own sphere of influence. To do so in 1965 would mean
acting with empathy toward "the slaves and their descendents"
by seeking justice at home with as much zeal as they might
seek it abroad.[22]

In asserting the importance of consistent commitment
to social justice in domestic as well as foreign affairs, Ellison

was extending perhaps the central aim of his politics: fighting for black freedom from the role of American scapegoat. This puts in mind Ellison's exchange with Robert Penn Warren, the former Southern Agrarian who in his youth had written an apology—albeit a half-hearted one—for segregation. Sounding as much a political tactician as an author, Ellison asserts, speaking of the civil rights movement:

> We want to socialize the cost. A cost has been exacted in terms of character, in terms of courage, and determination, and in terms of self-knowledge and self-discovery. Worse, it has led to social, economic, political, and intellectual disadvantages and to a contempt even for our lives. And one motive for our rejection of the old traditional role of national scapegoat is an intensified awareness that not only are we being destroyed by the sacrifice, but that the nation has been rotting at its moral core. Thus we are determined to bring America's conduct into line with its professed ideals. The obligation is dual, in fact mixed, to ourselves and to the nation. Negroes are forcing the confrontation between the nation's conduct and its ideal, and they are most American in that they are doing so.

Ellison's strong language of America as a nation "rotting at its core" expresses the sense of immediacy of political action that Ellison considers a necessity. Embodied within it is a barely contained rage, but also a directed sense of political purpose and acknowledgment of the necessity of sacrifice. As Danielle S. Allen observes, "The sacrifices of African Americans living in a segregated polity were sufficiently extreme to

constitute scapegoating in Ellison's terms rather than legiti-
mate sacrifice, and yet, he argued, they nonetheless revealed a
truth that applies to all democratic citizens: the political world
cannot be entirely separated from the social world, and learning how to negotiate the losses one experiences at the hands of
the public is fundamental to becoming a political actor, not
only for minorities suffering political abuses, but for all citizens." Far from aestheticizing politics to the point of abstrac-
tion, Ellison's assertions and, above all, his art point to pragmatic directions for political action.[23]

However, Ellison's zeal in his efforts to fight the scapegoating of blacks in the United States often occluded his vision
when it came to matters of global inequality and the United
States' quasi-imperialist actions in Vietnam. In this regard, Ellison may be guilty of lacking the simple but profound political insight of Muhammad Ali, who famously asserted in claiming his status as conscientious objector, "No Viet Cong ever
called me nigger." Ali paid the temporary price of his freedom
for his beliefs. Ellison, on the other hand, remained aloof on
the question of Vietnam even as he remained dedicated to the
cause of racial justice.

Ralph Ellison's faith in American democracy is all the more
striking when set against the dominant currents of black politics in the 1970s. In fiction and nonfiction, public and private
pronouncements, Ellison emerged as the foremost advocate
and most eloquent spokesman of the inextricable ties between
blacks and American democracy. Beginning with 1952's *Invisible Man*, most especially its striking epilogue, and stretching
into the expansive territory of his second novel some forty
years in progress, Ellison relentlessly pursued the challenge of
reconciling race and nation. In his nonfiction, he outlined his

evolving sense of pluralistic American culture and the unperfected promise of a multiracial American democracy. Ellison
understood that the ultimate responsibility of the American
writer was to "seize upon the abiding patterns of the American
experience as they come up within my own part of the American nation, and project those patterns, those personality
types, those versions of man's dilemmas, in terms of symbolic
actions."[24]

Ellison viewed the responsibility of the citizen to be similar to that of the artist: to extract from American experience
those elements that defined one's individual identity, then to
assert that individuality as a part of the collective. He articulated this ethic of citizenship in a 1970 interview with Russell
Kirk of WGBH radio in Boston.

> You can't have a divided society for over 300 years
> with the discriminated-against group developing
> some insights, some perceptions as to what is good
> for the entire society. You cannot live for 300 years
> in a state of cringing, certainly not in this democ-
> racy. You take what you can from the larger society,
> from its various styles, from its various idioms,
> from its various religions and you make something
> of yourself; you make something of it for yourself.
> This is one of the great promises of American life;
> this is how it actually works as against certain racist
> assumptions about how it works—and I stress
> assumptions. . . . We are a pluralistic society in ac-
> tuality, but we've been turning up too much of the
> feedback of the culture which should be applied by
> people who live out of a slightly different back-
> ground of tradition.

Ellison is not denying the pernicious effects of racism in America but rather asserting in the face of them his faith in American pluralism, not as the best way for American democracy, but as the only sustainable means. "This is a country wherein the man of imagination, the woman of imagination can abstract from the lifestyles of others, just as we abstract from the cuisine of all the world or the art of all the world," he continues, returning to his favored analogy between art and citizenship. "We make something new out of it, or at least, we appreciate it and play variations on it." Ellison understood Americans as riffers on reality rather than simply as pliant recipients of the status quo. Particularly for black Americans whose experience has conditioned them to necessary creativity, the task was clear: freedom ran through full acknowledgment of the rights and responsibilities of American citizenship.[25]

Ellison was a race man and an American patriot. That he could be both defies the limits by which each term is so often narrowly defined. The race man, a concept codified by St. Clair Drake and Horace Cayton in *Black Metropolis* (1945), identifies one who pursues race pride, race consciousness, and race solidarity. It is precisely this faith in the essential value of blacks to American democracy that inspired Ellison's love of country. Defying the jingoistic philosophy of "my country right or wrong," Ellison's patriotism predicated itself on an unstinting awareness of those wrongs, as well as an enduring faith in the nation's capacity to right them. His racial and national faiths defy easy resolution, instead calling for both affirmation and denial. In a letter to the editor of *Time* in 1958 responding to an article that had erroneously characterized his tenure at the American Academy in Rome as an "exile," he offered the following stern rebuke—also a clear articulation of how he con-

out his life, and even after his death, Ellison has been called an Uncle Tom and a race traitor for what his critics believe is his unwarranted faith in American democracy to right the wrongs against blacks. From the right, Ellison has been coopted by scholars such as Shelby Steele and Stephen and Abigail Thernstrom who distort Ellison's claims for black individual freedom to support simplistic bootstrap arguments for racial uplift and read his conflicted embrace of American identity as an untroubled acceptance of cultural assimilation.

What Ellison outlines in his essays and renders in his fiction, most powerfully in the numerous manuscript pages of his second novel, is a black American identity that defies such easy categorizations. The figure of the black American patriot, in all its complexity and seeming contradiction, offers a way into Ellison's thinking. It posits a host of challenges, many of which we have yet to face at the beginning of the twenty-first century.

Ellison's second novel likely came the closest it would ever come to completion in the early 1970s. Just a few years after the Plainfield fire in 1967, Ellison seems to have found renewed vigor and clarity of purpose. The novelist Leon Forrest offered a detailed assessment of the state of the novel in 1972, the very year Ellison seems to have completed revisions on his Book I and II typescripts. Forrest's insights are worth quoting at length:

> Ralph Ellison has been working for the last 17 years on what I believe is yet another major orchestra of a novel, actually going far past *Invisible Man,* in its larger than life dimensions concerning the American ethos. I have read perhaps five published chapters of the work-in-progress of this monumental work, reportedly measuring more than 1500 pages,

ceived of his racial and national identity: "I am too vindictive
American," he wrote, "too full of hate for the hateful aspects c
this country, and too possessed by the things I love about her,
to be too long away."[26]

Ellison was never long away from America, either in
physical proximity or in imaginative topography. Although the
etymology of patriotism asserts the love of country, Ellison's
vision is also motivated by hate, not of country, but rather of
those aspects of the country's practice that do harm to its
stated principles and to the people for which they stand. His is
more than a moralizing vision, however. Ellison does not rail
sternly against the nation's faults; rather, he draws from the
black vernacular tradition and, in particular, the tragicomic
sense to dramatize our national excesses and contradictions.
His America is both a projection of possibility and an ironic
critique of present-day reality. "One might indeed say that Ellison's version of America is created in the image of African-
American culture, not the other way around," Eric Lott argues.
"Life in Ellison's America has all the unexpected irony, clutch
self-reliance, and swinging resourcefulness of a tenor player
improvising on the wing." Lott does well to identify Ellison's belief in the vernacular wisdom of black culture. But Ellison would have rejected, I believe, the simplicity of Lott's rever-
sal. America is no more—and no less—a reflection of black culture than black culture is a reflection of America. The brilliance
of Ellison's black patriotic vision is that he refuses to elide the
dogged complexities and contradictions inherent in American
life: the beautiful absurdity of our American identity.[27]

Ellison's bold views have left him vulnerable to attacks
on multiple ideological fronts. From the left, he has been as-
sailed by Marxists and black nationalists who see his political
philosophy as capitulatory and his aesthetics as elitist. Through-

that he published in various magazines over the years. It is a work-in-progress that looks into patterns of sanity and continuity, the ruptured and chaotic memory of the national consciousness, and the moral responsibility for the past.

During a period of cheap, vogue-sustained Black writing, and patti-cake Jewish writing, and gross pornography, Ellison has been taking on the very deepest moral questions of the Union.[28]

In many ways Ellison's novel was atavistic, out of phase with a younger generation whose default posture was to reject tradition. Ellison saw in the confrontational posture of many in the younger generation of black Americans a willful negation of a legacy of black struggle and resiliency, immediately embodied in their parents' generation. He bemoaned the loss of nuance, the tenor of resignation and fear rendered as apathy, that he believed was epidemic among Black Power advocates. He understood himself to be writing in a period of momentous change, for black Americans and for the nation as a whole. He aimed for his fiction to reflect that change, to change as the world changed. In this capacity, Ellison was indeed in the vanguard of black leadership, albeit in the aesthetic rather than the political camp. Ellison typed the following on the back of a sheet of paper listing the course offerings from fall semester 1975, giving us a likely provenance for the note. It must be read, therefore, as a retrospective glance across nearly a decade, in a period in which Ellison was still often derided for his politics by a younger generation of black Americans.

Until the turbulent Sixties Negro Americans have lived by two principles, religion and aesthetics.

[They are] manifest in a ceaseless [sic] to impose their sense of style upon American life/ aesthetic drive created a profound sense of reality that was supported by a flexible sense of humor. Their religiosity gave sanction to their conception of their own humanity supported their faith in themselves, provided a sacred space, in Eliade's sense, that anchored their experience in a preChristian past and in a future that lay beyond the limits of death and dying. While their humor and aestheticism, mediating between the sacred and profane aspects of experience, served to define their complex humanity and affirm it against all the forces of society that would deny their humanity. But during the sixties that aestheticism and humor came under the attack of the nappyheaded generation which used it to reduce their parents['] cultural complexity to a simple-minded and reflexive racism.

Ellison's response to the oppositional stance taken by many in the younger generation began to take on the characteristics of an oppositional stance of his own. The result was not always productive for his fiction; it certainly did little for his popularity. For all of this, it is a testament to the broadness of Ellison's vision of America, to his appreciation for diversity, that his second novel would reflect a more empathetic understanding of later generations than notes like this would suggest. Ellison put all his hopes for the nation in his final novel. Increasingly, it seems that Ellison was coming to understand that the end he sought for his work in progress lay in the beginning of its conception, the putative year of the novel's setting: 1955.[28]

III

1955

By most accounts, 1955 marked the beginning of the civil rights movement. The Supreme Court, having handed down the landmark *Brown v. Board of Education* ruling overturning the separate but equal doctrine of *Plessy v. Ferguson* in 1954, now ordered that the nation's schools be integrated "with all deliberate speed." A host of other state and federal bodies followed suit, banning segregation in buses and railroad coaches and public recreational facilities. President Dwight D. Eisenhower issued Executive Order 10590 mandating nondiscriminatory practices in federal employment. And, most memorably, on December 1, Rosa Parks refused to relinquish her seat to a white man in the colored section of an Alabama bus, sparking the Montgomery bus boycotts and the emergence of a charismatic young minister, Martin Luther King, Jr.

That same year Ralph Ellison began his two-year tenure in Rome as a fellow at the American Academy of Arts and Letters, where he would dedicate himself to writing his second novel. It is difficult to conceive how this manuscript in progress could have been anything other than a novel of its time, this period in which the usual shifts in American culture and politics seemed to have risen to seismic proportions. In this era of national tumult—the burgeoning civil rights movement at home, the Cold War abroad—it seemed fitting that one of America's most acclaimed novelists would turn his attentions so deliberately to the political scene. Ellison wrote on May 19, 1954, to his former English teacher at Tuskegee, Morteza Sprague, that "the whole road [of postsegregationist America] stretched out and it got all mixed up with this book I'm trying to write and it left me twisted with joy and a sense of inadequacy." Ellison revealed that he was "writing about the evasion of identity which is another characteristically American problem which must be about to change. I hope so, it's giving me enough trouble." This sense of writing on the verge of dramatic change, of perhaps even contributing to that change, freighted Ellison's second novel with the heavy burden of history.[1]

The novel would be set "around 1955" and would move geographically from Georgia to Oklahoma to Washington, D.C.[2] Ellison explained to John Hersey in greater detail nearly twenty years later that the novel's time period runs "roughly from 1954 to 1956 or 1957. That is the time present in the novel, but the story goes back into earlier experiences, too, even to some of the childhood experiences of Hickman, who is an elderly man in time present. It's just a matter of the past being active in the present—or of the characters becoming aware of the manner in which the past operates on their present lives." Ellison held fast to this time period even as the decades passed. As a result, the manuscript would become temporally elastic, stretching to contain anachronisms in novelistic time that, in the writer's present, were simply part of the same ever-receding past. Historical events are fungible in Ellison's novel. "For here the novelist has a special, though difficult, freedom," Ellison explained to an interviewer in the 1970s. "Time is their enemy, and while chronology is the ally of the historian, for the novelist it is something to manipulate or even to destroy." One can see Ellison practicing this methodology throughout the second novel. His sense of history consists of those details that elucidate meaning rather than those that adhere slavishly to lived experience. This is evident, for instance, in his references to the lunar landing, to Afros, and to other details that are anachronistic for his putative 1955 setting. Their truth resides in another place, on the level of motif that is the province of the author of imaginative fiction.[2]

But it isn't what Ellison grafts onto the time period so much as what he takes away that is remarkable. At this moment of national foment in politics and in culture, Ellison renders a world surprisingly untroubled by the growing tensions forced on the American consciousness by segregation. Indeed, Ellison's second novel is often serene before the tumult of the era, curiously untouched by racial animus. Though much of the action takes place in the nation's capital, from the Lincoln and Jefferson Memorials to the Senate floor and Senate Office Building, the novel is strangely aloof from the political battles of the day. Hickman and his parishioners move freely through the capital, encountering only the occasional hindrance from whites: Miss Pryor, the Senator's Southern secretary, refuses to assist them; security guards subject them to an excessive search outside the Senate Office Building; a police lieutenant responds with bemusement on learning that the black people at Jessie Rockmore's mansion are tenants, not servants. Even these moments of racial bias prove occasions for comedy rather than critique. Ellison sketches these characters with a comic broadness, rendering them incapable of real harm. The result is that the novel evades the political and social costs of state-sanctioned racism in the form of segregation. As a political chronicler of this crucial period of our national life, it would seem that Ellison is missing in action.

Reflecting on *Invisible Man*, Arnold Rampersad remarks on a similar evasion of present-day political realities. "Major events and eras are ignored in *Invisible Man*," he writes. "The Depression is not identified. Allusions are made to World War I, but not to World War II. These omissions deliberately boost the allegorical element so important to [Ellison's] aims." For a novel such as *Invisible Man* whose aspirations lie in reifying the voice of a young black man to the level of the universal, such a method of strategic elision makes sense. But it is less clear from Ellison's own descriptions of his purpose in the second novel how effacing the complex racial terms of the historical present would further his novelistic aims. How can a novel set at the dawn of the civil rights movement lack a clear sense of racial struggle? How can an author so expressly committed to enacting in fiction America's internal crises of conscience and consciousness seem ultimately to resist the particulars of such a dynamic period in the nation's history?[3]

Ellison's fiction responds to these questions not by answering them but by transforming them. In the place where racism should be Ellison places assertions of black American identity. "After all, they are Americans," he writes in one form or another about his black characters throughout the novel. Ellison emphasizes the agency of black individuals against the efficacy of racism, either structural or personal. The result is a fictive world redolent of possibility and individual expression. Racism's most pernicious harm, Ellison seems to suggest, is to underestimate the black individual's equal claim to the dogged strength and creativity of the American character. Time and again Ellison renders scenes in which white characters—and sometimes black, though never Hickman—disregard the complexity, knowledge, or skill of black characters. This happens in the Rockmore scene where the white police refuse to believe that Jessie Rockmore could own the house and its many possessions, or at least own it without being a bootlegging criminal. It happens from the very beginning of the novel, when Senate security guards see Hickman and his congregation first as harmlessly comical, then as a potentially dangerous protest group, when they are neither. Each time Ellison underscores this mismeasure of black humanity with Hickman's ruminations on the American character and the particular complexity of black Americans tempered by the experience of racial prejudice.

The hallmark of the American character for Ellison is unexpectedness. In this regard, he owes a debt to Kenneth Burke, his philosophical mentor and frequent correspondent. In her study of their intellectual relationship, Beth Eddy characterizes their shared belief as such: "The level of *unexpectedness* a person ought to *expect* in the cultural milieu of the United States provides opportunities as well as dangers," she writes. "The sources of well-being for persons raised in a democratic climate are wider than what the family offers, but less predictable. Hence the uneasiness many people feel in acknowledging nonparental debts, which complicate a sense of personal and communal identity." Such unpredictability is at once the nation's greatest asset and sternest challenge. Although it endows the individual with at least the potential for boundless freedom, it risks ultimately ending in a nation of individuals distrustful of one another, particularly across racial lines.[4]

It is easy to slip from racial distrust to a protective racial zealotry, but Ellison's fiction also refuses this resolution. His purpose as a writer of fiction is not to incriminate the oppressor but to illuminate the victim's ability to escape victimization and create a life that is as defiantly proud, complex, and human as any other. This is a theme Ellison returns to often in his essays, and it takes many shapes in his fiction. Ellison's menagerie of characters includes a host of people who face limitations and outward constraints only to transcend them through creativity, conviction, and sheer will. Indeed, nowhere in the manuscript does Ellison ever credit racism with defeating any of his characters.

With the second novel Ellison has not written a fictional chronicle of the civil rights era such as Thulani Davis's *1959*, nor has he written a character-driven drama set against the backdrop of the time such as Charles Johnson's *Dreamer*. Instead, he offers a narrative that is unmistakably centered on the health of American democracy even as it portrays one of its most dramatic periods in the soft light of narrative remove. Ellison is at once the most overtly political of authors and yet the most reluctant to write political dogma. It would finally be this that would lead to charges of his being an Uncle Tom and of abandoning the fight for black freedom. Years later, when embroiled in his heated rhetorical battle with the Jewish critic Irving Howe over Howe's invidious comparison that pitted Ellison (and Baldwin) against Richard Wright, Ellison would articulate his vision of the writer's proper place in the struggle for black equality. At the end of a scathing response to Howe, Ellison appended the following open letter.

Dear Irving, I'm still yakking on and there's many thousand gone, but I assure you that no Negroes are beating down my door, putting pressure on me to join the Negro Freedom Movement, for the simple reason that they realize that I am enlisted for the duration. Such pressure is coming only from a few disinterested "military advisers," since Negroes want no more fairly articulate would-be Negro leaders cluttering up the airways. For, you see, my Negro friends recognize a certain division of labor among the members of the tribe. Their demands, like that of many whites, are that I publish more novels— and here I am remiss and vulnerable, perhaps.[5]

This public rendition of a personal communication articulates one of Ellison's core beliefs—that art is a form of political action, the only action his fellow black Americans ask of him and the only, perhaps, to which he is properly suited. Of course, neither was true. But in the distance between Ellison's assertion of the fact and its contradiction, we find Ellison's greatest vulnerability in his claim to being an American writer uniquely committed to American democracy and black freedom. What action does an active citizen—regardless of his or her professional calling—owe the nation? Does art alone suffice? And what must be the features of that art if it is to have political consequence? These questions animate the second novel during the critical decade between 1955 and 1965, the period that would witness the radical transformation of the American social compact.

"I am a novelist, not an activist but I think that no one who reads what I write or who listens to my lectures can doubt that I am enlisted in the freedom movement," Ellison told an interviewer in 1966 by way of responding to criticisms that he had not taken a more visible role in civil rights protests. "As an individual," he continues, "I am primarily responsible for the health of American literature and culture. When I write, I am trying to make sense out of chaos. To think that a writer must think about his Negroeness is to fall into a trap." Ellison ascribes for himself here the role of American literary custodian, charged with maintaining certain commitments that fall to any other artist writing out of the tradition of Walt Whitman, Herman Melville, and Frederick Douglass: to call the nation to account for the deficit between its principles and its practice, to ask and to begin answering the overarching moral questions of the day, and to help chart a course toward a democratic future that is in keeping with the nation's great promise. Given these lofty aims it does, indeed, seem somewhat petty to limit oneself to issues of race alone—as if they could be isolated in the first place.[6]

Yes, Ellison was writing a civil rights novel, but one that frames its protest in expressly aesthetic rather than nakedly political terms. On the back of an envelope postmarked February 5, 1965, just as the movement was reaching its climax, Ellison scrawled the following note, an essential clue to both his purpose and his practice: "Negroes must build upon the novel as the Civil Rights movement builds upon the constitution— or more precisely—as the Negro Civil Rights lawyers build upon the long and intricate tradition of constitutional law." In framing the analogy one can see Ellison's process of analytical refinement and revision at work. His first comparison is admittedly imprecise because it equates the concrete task of the black novelist to a pair of principles (the "movement" and the Constitution). His refinement of the comparison, on the other hand, makes a precise, if ambitious, claim for the black novelist's purpose: to put those principles into practice just as civil rights lawyers expand upon the given to achieve a broader context for freedom. The task for black novelists, then, is to build up from the limitations presented to them—not of the novel's form itself, which is infinite possibility, but of the inherited tradition of writing, which is the product of individuals— to achieve a liberated form that better accounts for the varieties of lived experience. In doing so, Ellison enlists himself in the broader struggle for black freedom, albeit on a distant front.[7]

In a 1965 interview, Richard Kostelanetz asked Ellison explicitly whether he believed a novelist could have "any great social reforming power or have any great expansive power or any great power as a spokesman." Ellison insisted in response that the novel is "a form of social action, and an important task. Yes, and in its own right a form of social power." That power, he argued, is achieved by extracting from lived experience certain "abiding patterns of human existence." "And when successful," Ellison continued, "he provides the reader with a fresh vision of reality. For then through the symbolic action of his characters and plot he enables the reader to share forms of experience not immediately his own." Central to the function of this process in his own fiction, particularly as the second novel is concerned, is Ellison's assertion of black people's centrality to any corporate American identity. Asserting human complexity against the mismeasure of black humanity, Ellison saw his fiction as enacting a powerfully democratic response to the calcified practices of segregated American life. Such work, Ellison suggested, requires a certain isolation on the part of the novelist from more immediate forms of social action and protest.[8]

Even if we accept the legitimacy of Ellison's aestheticized struggle, which many of his critics refused to do, important questions remain about the substance of Ellison's vision of black American life. Does he overestimate the black individual's ability to overcome segregation? Does he underestimate the harm inflicted on black Americans by slavery and white supremacy? In *Heroism and the Black Intellectual,* Jerry Gafio Watts answers both of these questions in the affirmative. Watts argues that Ellison's faith in black culture as power and his insistence on the Americanness of black individuals renders him myopic in the face of racism. "Ellison has woven an intellectual defense of black equality that appears to render any recognition of the detrimental impact of racism on black lives potentially threatening to the validation of Negro humanity," he writes. This "defense of black equality" takes shape in Ellison's assertion of American identity but also in his denial of racism's efficacy. "Ellison utilizes hegemonic American democratic rhetorics as well as the resilient hopeful outlooks of many black Americans to divert his attention from the most debilitating aspects of black existence in America." In other words, Watts sees Ellison's answer to racism as American patriotism. From the epilogue of *Invisible Man* through his classic essays of the 1950s and 1960s and beyond, Ellison would espouse a vision of black American patriotism tempered by the knowledge that America had yet to square its practice with its principles. By appealing to abstractions like the "principle" and the "sacred documents" of the nation's founding, by claiming "the Constitution as Ground or Scene for the Understanding of the Dreams of American Democracy" as he does in the notes for an unpublished essay, one wonders whether Ellison overcredits American principle with the power to shield blacks from American practice. Were Ellison's appeals to American principle and patriotism simply, in Watts's words, a diversion from the necessary task of achieving black freedom? Watts's critique is echoed by Cornel West, who praises Ellison's intellectual courage but chastises Ellison for becoming "such an American nationalist."[9]

Ellison would seem vulnerable to such criticisms that interpret his faith in American democratic principles as signaling a deficit of understanding toward the debilitating aspects of black existence. In *Democracy Matters,* Cornel West makes a significant distinction between naked patriotism and deep democracy. "Our history," he writes, "shows that stirring the deep commitment to democratic values and mandates does make a difference. But we must not confuse this democratic commitment with flag-waving patriotism. The former is guided by complex virtues forged by ordinary citizens, the later by martial ideals promoted by powerful elites. Democratic commitment confronts American hypocrisy and mendacity in the name of public interests; flag-waving patriotism promotes American innocence and purity in the name of national glory."[10]

Ellison's patriotism is far from naive, nor is it simply a cynical defense of American innocence. Quite the contrary, his is a tempered faith forged in the experience of the nation's failure to extend freedom to its black citizens. Far from an easy acceptance, Ellison's patriotism is the product of struggle with and against the nation. "I've never been able to dismiss democratic ideals so easily as have some of my colleagues whose racial background make the rewards of democracy more easily available," Ellison wrote in a letter to John Callahan in the 1980s. "Therefore I would affirm the principles while insisting that they be extended to all and on the basis of equality. It aint the theory which bothers me, [it's] the practice. My problem is to affirm while resisting." To affirm while resisting is the model of Ellison's patriotic ethic. It demands the exercise of faith, but also of discernment.[11]

Ellison would shape his belief in the unrealized promise

of American freedom into an statement of aesthetic purpose, a manifesto for black American fiction. In an undated note related to the second novel he makes a bold claim for black fiction, one that evinces not only an awareness of black struggle but a dogged assertion of the value of artistic creation as a means of liberation: "The Negro writer must be like a man with good eyesight who is forced by his knowledge of the reality of the U.S. to learn Braille, and who does indeed use it whenever things democratic become too cloudy. He clings to the promise desp[i]te the evidence of his eyes. Thus he clings to the evidence of his fingertips—a desperate but necessary extreme." In this powerful analogy Ellison speaks both to the general condition of black Americans in the era of segregation as well as to the specific circumstances of the black writer who, though endowed with acute vision, must confront the obscuring influence of American racism by adapting another mode of "seeing" beyond sight. This evocative phrase, "the evidence of his fingertips," is Ellison's assertion of the writer's essential capacity just as it is his admission of the desperation of social circumstance. It offers a powerful response to those who would presume that Ellison's patriotism signaled a retreat from experience. Like his famous definition of the blues as "an impulse to keep the painful details and episodes of a brutal experience alive in one's aching consciousness, to finger the jagged grain, and to transcend it, not by the consolation of philosophy but by squeezing from it a near-tragic, near-comic lyricism," Ellison's definition of black fiction relies on this same dual process of experience and transcendence. As a writer, Ellison's own process was necessarily mediated through the act of aesthetic creation.[12]

The connection Ellison would sometimes draw between politicians and writers went beyond analogy. Throughout his literary career, Ellison expounded on the importance of technique and tradition in both art and politics. This was particularly true, Ellison believed, for black Americans, be they artists or civic leaders. Late in his career, even as he continued to add to his novel set in the 1950s, he mused on the particular challenge facing the black artist. "How could the writer help our people out of a hole if he remained in the hole himself? How help lift the veil of ignorance form the eyes of others if we ourselves remained blind? Such questions were inescapable, because emotional relief aside, it would seem that talking constantly about race could no more make us artists than it could make aspiring physicians or champion athletes. And freedom, our grandparents' previous condition of servitude notwithstanding, lay in acquiring a command of techniques and a knowledge of tradition." Ellison's faith in the twin disciplines of technique and tradition undoubtedly stems in part from the perspective he had forged for himself through art. First through music and sculpture, later through photography and finally through fiction, Ellison found a way to enter the world as an equal by virtue of his achievement. This was a belief—at times it seems like fantasy—shared by many of his generation, that by dint of hard work and self-mastery, one could effect freedom. Ellison held to this view to the last, despite mounting evidence, particularly in the aftermath of the civil rights era that individual effort alone—mastery of technique and knowledge of tradition—was not enough to counteract ingrained structural inequality. "Even as an officially sanctioned apartheid was being dismantled," argues historian Nikhil Pal Singh, "new structures of racial inequality, rooted in national racial geography and urban ghettoes and suburban idylls, and intractable disparities of black and white wealth and employment were being established. For three decades, reformist and putatively race-neutral social policies formulated in the New Deal era actually reinforced and expanded numerous racial disparities." This is a reality that escapes Ellison's ethic of technique and tradition.[13]

Ellison's faith was both a generational one and a personal one, born of the hope of the civil rights movement and of the evidence of achievement Ellison saw in his own success as a Negro in the lily-white echelons of high culture. Returning once again to Ellison's letter to Morteza Sprague written just after *the Brown v. Board of Education* decision, one hears in Ellison's words an affirmation of democratic principle even as he resists democratic practice. "Well so now the Court found in our favor and recognized our human psychological complexity and citizenship and another battle of the Civil War has been won. The rest is up to us and I'm very glad," he writes, with a certain ironic regard for the necessity of the Court "recognizing" what is an inalienable right even as he asserts the responsibility of citizenship that comes with such rights and recognition. "The decision came while I was reading *A Stillness at Appomattox* and a study of the Negro Freedman," he continues, "and it made a heightening of emotion and a telescoping of perspective, yes and a sense of the problems that lie ahead that left me wet-eyed. I could see the whole road stretched out and it got all mixed up with this book I'm trying to write and it left me twisted with joy and a sense of inadequacy." Ever the man of letters, Ellison filters his understanding of this dramatic event through literature and then releases it through his writing. The "joy and inadequacy" he feels suggest that Ellison was far from aloof from his era; quite the contrary, it asserts how seriously he took his responsibility as a chronicler of this period, not in "historical terms" alone, but in the more impressionistic forms of fiction. The conclusion of the letter testifies to the depth of Ellison's relation to his time and to the seriousness with which he regarded his role as a writer. It may hint at why Ellison's second novel, despite all his engagement with the politics of his day, adopted a removed perspective from the explicit terms of racial struggle.

> Why did I have to be a writer during a time when events sneer at your efforts, defying consciousness and form? Well, so now the judges have found and Negroes must be individuals and that is hopeful and good. What a wonderful world of possibilities are unfolded for the children! For me there is still the problem of making meaning out of the past and I guess I'm lucky I described Bledsoe before he was checked out. Now I'm writing about the evasion of identity which is another characteristically American problem which must be about to change. I hope so, it's giving me enough trouble. Anyway, here's to integration, the only integration that counts: that of the personality.

Though the letter ends on an undeniable note of hope, Ellison's toast to integration, its gravity is unmistakable. Ellison phrases a challenge that he will echo throughout the decades as he labored on his second novel. The "aura of summing up" is the writer's response to the challenge of giving "consciousness and form" to swiftly changing circumstances—those events that "sneer at your efforts." Ellison found himself, therefore, drawn to the grand subject of the nation's shifting reality even as he looked with trepidation on the enormity of his avowed subject.[14]

Just as Ellison was coming to a more complex under-

standing of American freedom through the dramatic events of
the early civil rights movement, other black authors were head-
ing the other way—away from what they believed to be the unperfected promise of American democracy. W. E. B. Du Bois was
beginning to doubt the practicability of blacks finding freedom
in the United States, spurring him to seek new possibilities in
Pan-Africanism. Similarly, from France Richard Wright was
advocating a radical rejection not simply of American national
bonds but of all communal bonds. Writing in the foreword to
George Padmore's *Pan-Africanism or Communism* in 1956,
Wright asserts the following, in dramatic contrast to the sense
of promise Ellison expressed in his letter to Sprague:

> Oppression oppresses, and this is the conscious-
> ness of black men who have been oppressed for
> centuries,—oppressed for so long that their oppres-
> sion has become a tradition, in fact, a kind of cul-
> ture. This elementary fact baffled white men, Com-
> munist and non-Communist alike, for more than
> fifty years. The Negro's outlook is basically deter-
> mined by his economic and social position, by his
> colour, and racial oppression. The Negro did not
> create the issue of colour, or race, or the condition
> in which he lives, but he has been moulded and
> influenced by them. The Negro's fundamental loy-
> alty is, therefore, to *himself*. His situation makes
> this inevitable. (Am I letting awful secrets out of the
> bag? I'm sorry. The time has come for this problem
> to be stated clearly so that there is no possibility of
> further misunderstanding or confusion. The Negro,
> even when embracing Communism or Western
> Democracy, is not supporting ideologies; he is seek-

ing to use *instruments* (instruments owned and controlled by men of other races!) for his own ends. He stands outside of those instruments and ideologies; he has to do so, for he is not allowed to blend with them in a natural, organic and healthy manner.)

Wright's statement is striking, not simply in its bold assertion of black self-interest, that "the Negro's fundamental loyalty is . . . to *himself*," but in extending that philosophy to suggest that "even when embracing Communism or Western Democracy," the black individual is still a nationality unto him- or herself. Denying a black stake in established ideologies, Wright even rejects black control of the instruments of ideology that might be turned to other means. In effect, then, Wright seems to be arguing for blacks resigning themselves from politics entirely (from the instrumentation of ideology) in favor of a life outside social compacts. The irony of this argument in light of his 1953 novel, *The Outsider*, in which Wright renders a black character, Cross Damon, who proves the impossibility of "standing outside" political and social institutions, seems to have escaped Wright. Perhaps part of what made Wright so appealing to blacks in the years following the civil rights era was that he modeled a way of opting out of American politics and society. For his part, Ellison refused to relinquish black claims to both the ideology and the instruments of American democracy. The novel that was only now taking shape would assert beyond all challenges from without or desires from within that the fate of black Americans was not only bound up with, but would in fact help dictate, the fate of the nation.[15]

> This was the American dream: a sanctuary on the earth for individual man: a condition in which he

could be free not only of the old established closed-
corporation hierarchies of arbitrary power which
had oppressed him as a mass, but free of that mass
into which the hierarchies of church and state has
compressed and held him individually thrilled and
individually impotent.

We will establish a new land where man can assume that every individual man—not the mass of
men but individual man—has an inalienable right
to individual dignity and freedom within a fabric of
individual carriage and honorable work and mu-
tual responsibility.

—William Faulkner, "On Privacy:
The American Dream"

In "Tell It Like It Is, Baby," an essay composed in 1956 but
left unfinished and unpublished until 1965, Ellison asserts that
desegregation demonstrates the "clash between the American
dream and everyday American reality," between the ideals es-
poused in our founding documents and the lived experience
of thirteen million black Americans. "And even in so practical
and (until recently) so far removed an area as that of foreign
policy," Ellison continues, "does not this clash, especially when
we regard Asia and Africa, make for an atmosphere of dream-
like irrationality?" In the face of such irrationality, we are re-
minded that the very foundational terms of our republic are
in constant flux—equality, liberty, democracy. "Even the word
'democracy'—the ground-term of social rationality, the rock
upon which our society was built—changes into its opposite,"
Ellison writes, "depending upon who is using it, upon his
color, racial identity, the section of the country in which he
happened to have been born, or where and with whom he hap-

pens to be at the moment of utterance." This conditionality of American democratic freedom remains an unwanted reality for a nation that wished to portray itself as the beacon of liberty for the world or, in Faulkner's words, a "sanctuary on earth for individual man." Langston Hughes's long poem "Let America Be America Again" told another story: while America may have indeed been "the dream the dreamers dreamed," it was never so for all, it was never so for him.[16]

As an American novelist, it was Ellison's self-ascribed task to expose and to dramatize these constantly shifting forces and meanings. Though he was committed to American principles, he was nonetheless cognizant of the long-standing American practice of scapegoating. Black Americans had long served as a counterweight to the freedom of white Americans. Ellison saw in the civil rights movement a necessary rejection of this insuperable practice. "We want to socialize the cost," he explained to Robert Penn Warren in 1965. "A cost has been exacted in terms of character, in terms of courage, and determination, and in terms of self-knowledge and self-discovery. Worse, it has led to social, economic, political, and intellectual disadvantages and to a contempt even for our lives. And one motive for our rejection of the old traditional role of national scapegoat is an intensified awareness that not only are we being destroyed by the sacrifice, but that the nation has been rotting at its moral core. Thus we are determined to bring America's conduct into line with its professed ideals. The obligation is dual, in fact mixed, to ourselves and to the nation. Negroes are forcing the confrontation between the nation's conduct and its ideal, and they are most American in that they are doing so." This idea of a dual obligation, far from simply a matter of blaming the victim, is rather a claim to empowerment—that black people, too, had some control over their own fate, that freedom was not simply to be given but to be won. The American Dream, then, for Ellison was embodied in the struggle to "bring America's conduct into line with its professed ideals" through the dual exercise of national and individual power.[17]

A few years before, near the height of the civil rights movement in 1961, Martin Luther King, Jr., cast black American freedom in much the same terms. In an address on "The American Dream," he voiced a prophetic warning that extends Ellison's assertion of the "clash between the American dream and everyday American reality": "The price America must pay for the continued exploitation of the Negro and other minority groups is the price of its own destruction. The hour is late; the clock of destiny is ticking out. It is trite, but urgently true, that if America is to remain a first-class nation she can no longer have second-class citizens. Now, more than ever before, America is challenged to bring her noble dream into reality, and those who are working to implement the American dream are the true saviors of democracy." Both Ellison and King predicated their appeal for racial equality on American patriotism. The United States, they both posit, is a nation of liberty committed to a set of lofty principles even if our practice has often ignored them. "Indeed," King asserted, "slavery and segregation have been strange paradoxes in a nation founded on the principle that all men are created equal." Ellison and King, in other words, both wield the rhetoric of American democratic principle as a cudgel against the racism rampant in the practice of American life. This is not to say that their appeals to principle are merely rhetorical but rather that they both saw rhetoric, and specifically the rhetoric of democratic freedom, as essential to achieving a liberated reality for black Americans.[18]

The dominant rhetoric of the early civil rights movement drew on American patriotism to define the terms of freedom. In asserting the significance of language in the struggle both Ellison and King extend a tradition that, in the African-American grain, extends backward to slavery and abolitionism. On July 5, 1852, Frederick Douglass delivered an address sponsored by the Rochester Ladies' Anti-Slavery Society to commemorate the signing of the Declaration of Independence. Using this high point of American patriotic celebration as his touchstone, Douglass voices a striking polemic on passion as well as principle. Part rebuke, part appeal, the speech leaves unreconciled the dichotomies of black and white, slave and citizen. "What, to the American slave, is your 4th of July?" he asks. Douglass's response is that it means precious little indeed as long as the nation's actions pervert its principles.[19]

Douglass's very diction embodies this ambivalent relationship to the United States. He speaks to his predominantly white audience about "your political freedom," "your great deliverance," and "your national life," but he also calls them "Fellow Citizens." Indeed, the tone he establishes at the outset of the speech is inviting, partaking of the conventional habits of patriotic speechmaking. He goes so far as to argue that it is right and fitting for his audience to celebrate Independence Day. "Pride and patriotism," he says, "not less than gratitude, prompt you to celebrate and to hold it in perpetual remembrance. I have said that the Declaration of Independence is the ringbolt to the chain of your nation's destiny; so, indeed, I regard it. The principles contained in that instrument are saving principles. Stand by those principles, be true to them on all occasions, in all places, against all foes, and at whatever cost." Douglass is not suing for emancipation here; he is not chastising or even using moral suasion to convince his audience to oppose slavery. Rather, he is establishing both the history of the nation's founding and its adherence to principle. He does this, of course, with the intention of setting up a distinct contrast with the loss of that principle in the institution of slavery, but he nonetheless shows an uncommon patience in extenuating this patriotic set-up. In a remarkable series of rhetorical questions, Douglass phrases the same challenges that Ralph Ellison will still be raising a hundred years later in the epilogue of *Invisible Man*.

> Fellow-citizens, pardon me, allow me to ask, why am I called upon to speak here to-day? What have I, or those I represent, to do with your national independence? Are the great principles of political freedom and of natural justice, embodied in the Declaration of Independence, extended to us? and am I, therefore, called upon to bring our humble offering to the national altar, and to confess the benefits and express devout gratitude for the blessings resulting from your independence to us?
>
> Would to God, both for your sakes and ours, that an affirmative answer could be truthfully returned to these questions!

Douglass rejects the possibility of black patriotism, of making an "offering to the national altar," not for lack of will or desire, but for lack of access to the freedoms befitting an American patriot. He casts his rejection of the responsibilities and the offices of active citizenship not in terms of anger or revolt but in terms of incapacity. It is a call to action phrased in an appeal to the ideals of patriotic brotherhood.[20]

Douglass's speech closes with a rhetorical knockout punch after the setup offered by his praise of American democracy and independence. One can read it as a kind of alternative declaration of independence for enslaved black Americans. "Standing there identified with the American bondman," he says, "making his wrongs mine, I do not hesitate to declare, with all my soul, that the character and conduct of this nation never looked blacker to me than on this 4th of July!" Douglass's diction is purposeful; he ironically employs "blacker" to signify moral culpability and decay on one side as well as the dogged presence of enslaved black Americans on the other. He also proffers the damning contrast between past principle and present action. "Whether we turn to the declarations of the past," he continues, "or the professions of the present, the conduct of the nation seems equally hideous and revolting. America is false to the past, false to the present, and solemnly binds herself to be false to the future. Standing with God and the crushed and bleeding slave on this occasion, I will, in the name of humanity which is outraged, in the name of liberty which is fettered, in the name of the Constitution and the Bible which are disregarded and trampled upon, dare to call in question and to denounce, with all the emphasis I can command, everything that serves to perpetuate slavery—the great sin and shame of America!" In this high-toned passage, Douglass delivers perhaps his most stinging rebuke of American practice. Affirming the principle, he denies the crimes and sins of those who perpetuate the system of slavery. Douglass invokes, in equal measure, secular and sacred judgment.[21]

Ellison never reaches Douglass's pitch of critique and outrage. He does, however, share Douglass's sense of alienation. In an early essay, "Harlem Is Nowhere," Ellison describes the peculiar position of those poor blacks living on the night-side of American freedom. "Not quite citizens and yet Americans, full of the tensions of modern man but regarded as primitives," he writes, "Negro Americans are in desperate search for an identity. Rejecting the second-class status assigned them, they feel alienated and their whole lives have become a search for answers to the questions: Who am I, What am I, Why am I, and Where?" In a land marked by freedom and opportunity, those kept out feel an intensity of resentment in direct relation to their proximity to that freedom. The result, Ellison argued, was a peculiar condition of the black psyche that made it impossible to share in the celebration and exaltation of American democracy.

> When Negroes are barred from participating in the main institutional life of society, they lose far more than economic privileges or the satisfaction of saluting the flag with unmixed emotions. They lose one of the bulwarks which men place between themselves and the constant threat of chaos. For whatever the assigned function of social institutions, their psychological function is to protect the citizen against the irrational, incalculable forces that hover about the edges of human life like cosmic destruction lurking within an atomic stockpile. And it is precisely the denial of this support through segregation and discrimination that leaves the most balanced Negro open to anxiety.
>
> Though caught not only in the tensions arising from his own swift history, but in those conflicts created in modern man by a revolutionary world, the Negro cannot participate fully in the therapy which the white American achieves through patriotic ceremonies and by identifying himself with American wealth and power. Instead, he is thrown back upon his own 'slum-shocked' institutions.

The very denial of patriotism renders black Americans without the necessary democratic support of optimism, that sense of promise even under the most abject conditions. Standing outside the democratic compact, they engender a conflicted and even hostile relationship to the nation that refuses to extend to them the same promises and protections of full citizenship. This is where the racial difference comes into play. For even poor whites, by the very fact of their whiteness, were initiated into at least the promise of American wealth and power. Hence, we have seen that those who have suffered most from American capitalism have ironically been most invested in its ethos, if only for the promise of mercurial success. This is at least one definition of the American Dream.[22]

Ellison's vision of American patriotism, one that would suffuse his second novel, is grounded in—but not bounded by—an explicitly African-American tradition of protest. Undoubtedly Ellison would have bristled at what he might have perceived as such a reductive definition of his art, but it is a necessary corrective to those who would claim the substance of Ellison's beliefs as somehow an outlier from the black tradition. It is rather in his execution of those beliefs in the particular contours of his fiction, not his appeal to American patriotism itself, in which Ellison distinguishes himself from both tradition and the civil rights era from which his novel is born.

When asked in 1965 why he had not yet published his novel in progress, Ellison responded with disarming candor. "Well, it takes me a long time because I have a deep uncertainty about what I am doing," he said. "I try to deal with large bodies of experience which I see as quite complex. There is such a tendency to reduce the American experience, especially when it centers around the Negro experience. I'm constantly writing—I write a lot—but I have put it aside. It has to gel, then I come back. If I still react positively to it, if I can still see possibilities of development, then I keep it." In light of the three decades that would follow this statement without a published novel, Ellison's response takes on even greater significance. Ellison's uncertainty, it seems, sprang not from lack of faith in his craft or confusion over his aesthetic vision but rather from the self-imposed burden of his ambitious aim to "deal with large bodies of experience." Perhaps the greatest of these experiences is the civil rights movement, which exists in the manuscripts not in explicit terms but in the very attitude of his fiction: the bold assertion of black Americans' complex humanity and their centrality to national, and even global, affairs.[23]

Ellison enacts in his second novel the drama of the civil rights era without so much as describing a single protest. How can America save itself from the betraying its own most sacred principles? Alonzo Hickman's struggle, like that of the authentic (black) patriot, is to keep faith in that which seems to have forsaken him, be it a child or a nation. He follows this path not out of blind faith or abject submission but in the knowledge that it presents the last, best hope for the future. The central drama of the novel in progress, the estrangement and reconciliation of fathers and sons, is also a signal drama of the American experience.

The story of Bliss's birth, recounted in a manuscript fragment Ellison titled by that name, sets forth the terms of tragic circumstance at the center of Hickman and Bliss's relationship. His brother lynched after being falsely accused of raping a white girl, his mother dead from the shock, Hickman barricades himself in his childhood home, waiting for a lynch mob to exact its revenge on him, too. Instead, the girl herself arrives, nearly ready to deliver the child that indirectly had become the

source of all this death. Resisting the urge to seek his own revenge, Hickman responds to the challenge of circumstance,
helping to deliver the child. In an act that seems more ritual
than reality, the mother leaves the child in Hickman's care as a
strange recompense for what he has lost. "After what I've
done," she explains, "you'll need to have him as much as I need
to give him up. Take him, let him share your Negro life and
whatever it is that allowed you to help us all these days. Let him
learn to share the forgiveness your life has taught you to
squeeze from it. . . . And you'll need him to help prevent you
from destroying yourself with bitterness. With me he'll only be
the cause of more trouble and shame and later it'll hurt him."
Almost as soon as Bliss is born, he has become a child of salvation. At first, his salvific power is personal: he is vested with
the power to save both his now-absent mother and his surrogate father from their respective fates. "I thought, *I'll call him
Bliss, because they say that's what ignorance is,*" Hickman explains. "Yes, and little did I realize that it was the name of the
old heathen life I had already lost." Bliss draws Hickman out of
his life of dissolution, redirecting him toward devotion, both
to God and to the child he gives a name. As Ellison would explain in a typed note, "Bliss symbolizes for Hickman an American solution as well as a religious possibility. Hickman thinks
of Negroes as the embodiment of American democratic promises, as the last who are fated to become the first, the down-
trodden we who shall be exalted." Expressing democratic faith
in Christian terms, Ellison endows Bliss and Hickman's relationship with rich implications.[24]

Hickman's transformation from jazz man to man of God
corresponds with Bliss's transformation from agent of personal salvation to agent of collective salvation. Born of indeterminate race but raised as black, he represents Ellison's cen-

tral assertion of American identity in the flesh: that "whatever else the true American is, he is also somehow black." The child soon emerges as a vouchsafe for the black folk among whom he is raised of the unrealized promise of their freedom. "He was our young hope," Hickman explains years later from the hospital bed of the Senator, the man Bliss somehow has become, "our living guarantee that you still spoke to us and gave down your promise even in our hardest times. Now just look at him, all ravaged by his denials, sapped by his running away, twitching like a coke fiend from his twistings and turnings." In the transmogrification of Bliss's identity to Sunraider, in the very mortification of his flesh, Ellison refashions the New Testament story of salvation for modern-day America. "You don't reject Jesus because somebody calls Joseph a confidence man or Mary a whore; the spears and the cross and the crime were real and so was the pain," he continues, making explicit the comparison he wishes to establish between Bliss and Christ. But it is too simplistic to say that Bliss is a "Christ figure" or that we are to read his fate in terms of the grand biblical narrative alone. Indeed, Bliss's story is marked by the particulars of the American experience, of slavery and freedom, failure and promise.[25]

The child Bliss emerges in the typescripts of Ellison's second novel as rebuke and salvation for a nation in crisis. Although the typescripts would leave him suspended on the edge of death, it would not push him over. His life, as tenuous as it is, affirms Ellison's hope in the neglected promise of the nation finally perfecting the practice of its multiracial democracy. In this regard, Bliss represents America's racial and cultural fusion in the flesh.

> A marvelous child of Ishmaelian origin and pariah's caste, but his blending of bloods and unusual expe-

rience endowed that child with a command of the
Word which was so inspiring that we came to accept him as the living token and key to that world
of togetherness for which our forefathers long hoped
and prayed. And since that child landed among us
during a time of great trouble we saw in him an answer to our hopes that this divided land with its diversity of people would at last be made whole. Yes,
and instilled with our own stubborn vision and
blues-tempered acceptance of this country's turbulent reality.

This is not a philosophy of assimilation but one of transfiguration. Ellison asserts that the body politic must not only accept
blacks, but allow itself to be transformed by the particulars of
the black experience. Bliss would bring about that "longed-for
transcendence of the past which would free us" not as a symbol alone, but as mechanism for an essential fusion; he is, as
Hickman calls him, "both symbol and spokesman." "And since
attaining the freedom to be our own unique selves while
peacefully coexisting with those who outnumbered us would
unify our goals, both religious and social," he continues, "we
rejoiced and gave thanks to the Lord for the sheer existence of
our rare gifted child." Freedom of self expression coupled with
peaceful coexistence unifies purpose. Such unity is also one of
the sacred and secular, of Scripture and Constitution. For
Hickman and his followers—and for the nation, Ellison suggests, more generally—losing Bliss means losing an opportunity, but not sacrificing faith. "So the blow was shattering, yes!
But the dream itself continued to haunt us, as it does to this
day, here in the vastness of Washington." In this line Ellison
reasserts the sense of undaunted hope that would prove the
resonant tone of his unfinished opus. In it, he would phrase a

response to the lingering question of his first novel's protagonist; here he would find a voice that could somehow speak for
us all. This is Ellison's true legacy: his unflagging commitment
to a nation forever in progress. It is the tie that binds this
unfinished second novel with *Invisible Man* and demands that
we return to the earlier novel's own evolving form to find
the true measure of Ellison's vision for the novel and for the
nation.[26]

Part II

IV

1952

Buried among the hundreds of notes Ralph Ellison jotted on loose scraps of paper, in spiral-bound notebooks, and on the backs of used envelopes is a small composition book of the kind familiar to most college students. On the line after "Property of" Ellison has scrawled his name and after "Subject" he has written a description of the journal's contents: "NOVEL: Opus II." This by itself is unremarkable. After all, Ellison kept copious notes throughout the second novel's extended gestation. They would provide the germ of his plot and the intimations of his most evocative phrases. This particular notebook, however, contains something extraordinary: possible evidence that Ellison conceived the broad contours of his second novel even before his first novel was finished. Although the notebook is undated, it bears a clue as to its provenance: Ellison has crossed out his address on St. Nicholas Avenue, replacing it with his new address on Riverside Drive, a move he made in the fall of 1952 when *Invisible Man* was already a best seller and Ellison was well on his way to becoming a literary celebrity.[1]

Such a seemingly inconsequential detail like a change of address matters because it suggests a private history of the second novel that conflicts with the public one Ellison would frequently provide in the years that followed. His public account of the novel's genesis emphasized its distance from *Invisible Man*. When Ellison spoke of his second novel's birth, he most often spoke of Rome. "I was pretty depleted by *Invisible Man*," he told John Hersey in 1982, "so I didn't start on another book immediately. I played around with various ideas and spent some time trying to salvage material I had edited out of *Invisible Man*. It was in Rome, during 1956, that I began to think vaguely about this book and conceived the basic situation, which had to do with a political assassination; this was involved with the other patterns—the coffin business." The "coffin business," the story of Jessie Rockmore, does indeed seem to have come to Ellison during his first year in Rome. But it appears certain that he conceived the "basic situation," including the political assassination, years earlier. Ellison's mythology has been so persuasive that even one of his closest literary confidants, Albert Murray, has written that it was "in Rome that he invented the crucial episode of the assassination in the Senate Chamber," a contention echoed by numerous others. The Opus II notebook clearly suggests that Ellison conceived the assassination and other critical plot details years before his departure for Rome.[2]

By dating the birth of the second novel after *Invisible Man*'s publication, even locating its conception a continent away, Ellison effectively created a line of demarcation designed to deflect any comparisons between the two works. He had done something similar in describing *Invisible Man*'s origins, mythologizing the arrival of the "disembodied voice" of his protagonist announcing "I am an Invisible Man," interrupting his work on his prisoner of war novel. As Ellison biographer

Arnold Rampersad has demonstrated, though, the line seems to have come to Ellison under far less dramatic circumstances than Ellison would suggest in his introduction to the thirtieth anniversary edition of the novel. Of course, one can hardly fault a writer of fiction for telling a good tale about his own story, even if that tale takes certain liberties with the truth. Such literary white lies are common. The small notebook refuses to go away, however; it insists on asserting not only an authentic narrative of the second novel's composition in all its complexity but also an indelible connection between Ellison's manuscript-just-in-progress and the one that was even then nearing the end of its six-and-a-half-year composition.[3]

Recounting the full history of the second novel's birth is not simply a matter of biographical fidelity; more significantly, it is an act of literary archaeology that restores the second novel to its proper imaginative context. It matters that the second novel took its form out of the swirl of activity in these last months of *Invisible Man*'s composition. It matters because it suggests, regardless of the specific connections between the texts, that Ellison's two novels were in conversation about a shared set of themes. That conversation reads like a call and response, a dialogue that would continue for the rest of Ellison's life.

Uncovering the roots of the second novel leads to Ellison's private communications rather than to his more guarded and strategic public pronouncements. In the early 1950s Ellison carried on vibrant correspondence about his works in progress (both *Invisible Man* and later the second novel) with a circle of literary peers, including Albert Murray, Stanley Edgar Hyman, Kenneth Burke, and a handful of others. In the years following *Invisible Man,* this circle would expand to include, at different times, Anatole Broyard, Saul Bellow, and William Styron. But it was Murray with whom Ellison shared the most about the second novel in the formative years of its composition. Over a series of letters spanning most of the decade, Ellison records his progress on the second novel in revealing, if sporadic, detail. The first of these letters is dated May 14, 1951, when Ellison wrote Murray a brief note from St. Nicholas Avenue stating that he was "trying to get started on my next novel (I probably have enough stuff left from the other if I can find the form)." A month later, on June 6, he wrote Murray a longer letter, mostly about the painstaking process of revising *Invisible Man*, that mentioned "trying to get going on my next book before this one is finished." These letters corroborate what the Opus II notebook demonstrates in print: that by the early 1950s the second novel was already evolving in Ellison's imagination, not distinct from but related to *Invisible Man*.[4]

In writing about this very notebook, Ellison biographer Lawrence Jackson asserts that Ellison "drafted the outline and wrote a notebook full of plot summaries for what became *Juneteenth*." Certainly the notebook includes plot outlines, though none of them would prove to be *the* outline; indeed, only a handful of scenes would find their way into the Book I and II typescripts from the 1970s and the computer sequences from the 1980s and 1990s, the two periods in which Ellison made concerted efforts to gather his various episodes into a novel. Over the forty-year composition, Ellison wrote hundreds of additional notes, sometimes developing but often superseding those from the notebook. The revelatory nature of the notebook's contents lies in the myriad connections Ellison was then conceiving between *Invisible Man* and his next book. It may be too much to say that the second novel was born out of *Invisible Man*, but it is nonetheless clear that Ellison had the themes and even particular characters of his first novel well in mind as he began writing what he would call his second opus.[5]

The clearest and most provocative thread connecting Ellison's two novels may be the elusive character from *Invisible Man* that proves critical for Ellison's nameless protagonist as the novel draws to its conclusion, B. P. Rinehart. Rinehart's connection to the second novel is most apparent in an expurgated scene from *Invisible Man* in which Ellison's protagonist seeks information about Rinehart from Julius Franklin, a Brother from the Harlem office. Julius tells the narrator that Rinehart had been a boy preacher and then the narrator muses that Rinehart might be the same as "another boy preacher who had grown up and passed for white and become. . . a reactionary writer on politics—with no one except a few negroes the wiser." Like Leroy, a character I shall discuss in Chapter 6, who would disappear, reappear, then reappear again (in the second novel), Rinehart too is reborn in Ellison's novel in progress, transformed and transfigured. Ellison's Opus II composition book makes it clear that the second novel belongs to "Rhinehart," as he spells the name throughout. Bliss Proteus Rhinehart is the hidden name and complex fate of this transitional character belonging both to *Invisible Man* and to the second novel, and yet to neither. In *Invisible Man* Rinehart had been Ellison's master of chaos. In the second novel, he would be the fulcrum around whom Ellison would conceive a story of fathers and sons, memory and rejection, fidelity and betrayal.[6]

As initially imagined in these notebook pages, Ellison's second novel explores a landscape of American chaos with Rhinehart as the central character. As Ellison actually began writing the novel, Rhinehart would go by other names—first Bliss, the child evangelist of indeterminate race whom a former jazzman turned preacher named Alonzo Hickman raises as his own; then Movie Man, an itinerant scam artist who arrives in a small Oklahoma town to film a movie, only to con the locals out of money; and finally Adam Sunraider, a "race-baiting New England Senator" who would ultimately be struck down by a part of his own past, a shot fired by his estranged son, a child conceived years before during his travels in that small Oklahoma town. In the Book II typescripts that comprise *Juneteenth*, Bliss/Sunraider emerges as the central voice, alongside Hickman, of Ellison's fiction. Existing mostly through his thoughts as he comes in and out of consciousness, in and out of the past, from the hospital bed where he lies critically wounded, it is clear that whatever else Ellison was writing, he was writing Bliss's story.

Bliss/Sunraider remains a central character in Ellison's fiction through most of the typescripts, though he is matched, and finally eclipsed, in importance by Hickman. Following the second novel's compositional history to the end, however, something almost inconceivable happens. Bliss all but disappears from the novel. As Ellison shifted work on the book to his computer, he also seems to have shifted his conception of his fiction away from Bliss. Although Bliss/Sunraider remains the putative motivation for the actions of other characters—notably Hickman, his estranged surrogate father, and Severen, his estranged son and assassin—he never appears in the narrative. Instead, he has been reduced largely to a plot device, less character himself than motivation for the actions of others.

It seems only fitting that a character capable of such radical transformations and subject to such changes from outside as well, would bear a name so loaded with symbolic meaning. Bliss Proteus Rinehart. The novel itself would take on the Protean cast of its first protagonist. Just as Bliss would find himself usurped by other more dominant characters, first Cliofus, the teller of tall tales, then Hickman, so too would Ellison's various conceptions of the manuscript itself shift and change. It may finally be that Bliss is too freighted with myth and symbolism; perhaps he stood for so much that Ellison could no longer endow him with life. Reading his flamboyant speech that begins *Juneteenth*, it seems that Sunraider—and perhaps Ellison with him—has fallen victim to his own symbolic rhetoric. Phrases that would easily find a home in one of Ellison's most earnest essays in defense of American complexity are now voiced by a character staunchly opposed to black equality. Undoubtedly one hears something of Ellison's deep irony, the "joke" he spoke so often about at the center of American experience, and yet one also senses a tone of fatigue, a ponderousness that weighs down the fiction. Whether Ellison sensed the same or not, it is clear that as the novel progressed, Bliss/Sunraider's role diminished in ways impossible to imagine in the earliest conceptions of the fiction.

Reading Rhinehart back into Bliss/Sunraider, as the journal invites us to do, may provide a way of reading forward as well, of understanding why a character so fundamental to the fiction for so many years would end up as little more than a plot device. At the same time, it may help us to understand what Ellison sought in his final conception of the novel and why he seems to have thought that focusing on Sunraider would somehow preclude it. Although Sunraider's role would gradually diminish, Rinehart's would remain, if only in spirit. An agent of transformation, Bliss Proteus Rinehart is a metaphor for the second novel as a whole, a way of explaining how Ellison could write for forty years without finishing his novel.

"Rinehart, Rinehart, I'm a most indiff'rent guy"
—"Harvard Blues"

> "Rinehart, Rinehart, I thought, what kind of man is
> Rinehart?"
>
> —*Invisible Man*

Rinehart, like so many of Ellison's characters, bears a name with a past. This past begins with a blues song written for Count Basie's orchestra and recorded with Ellison's old Oklahoma City friend Jimmy Rushing on vocals. "Harvard Blues" is admittedly something of a novelty number; it relates the trials and tribulations of a Harvard undergraduate, not the lives and loves of a hardscrabble bluesman. The song's brilliance lies in this ironic juxtaposition of form and content, a classic blues with a decidedly unbluesworthy subject. Lyricist and composer George Frazier drew on his own experience as a Harvard student in the late 1920s and early 1930s, layering the lyrics with insider references to Harvard's *Rules Relating to College Studies,* its Finals Clubs, and other fragments of its insular lore. Rinehart was a part of this hidden history, his name a "traditional signal for impromptu brawls and minor riots on the Harvard campus for more than half a century." Several versions of the term's origins exist, but the most compelling relates the story of a student named James B. G. Rinehart who, in a gambit to increase his popularity, took to calling his own name from outside his dormitory window. When his classmates discovered his secret, his name became a mocking and playful call to revel. The cry would soon be heard from Cambridge to Cairo.[7]

Ellison's own first encounter with Rinehart recalls a different set of lyrics than the ones Rushing recorded. Only after *Invisible Man*'s publication was he made aware of the coded meaning of the name, a detail he found particularly fitting given the riot in Harlem that follows on Rinehart's introduction. What captured Ellison about Rinehart was an inexorable quality in the name itself and in the way Rushing sang it. "My old Oklahoma friend, Jimmy Rushing, the blues singer," Ellison explains, "used to sing one with a refrain that went: Rinehart, Rinehart/ It's so lonesome up here/ On Beacon Hill." Perhaps the difference between the lyrics Frazier wrote (and Rushing sang on record) and the ones Ellison recalls can be explained by a lapse in Ellison's memory or maybe even attributed to a Rushing improvisational riff. Regardless, the name and the refrain remain. Rinehart, Ellison reveals, "haunted me, and as I was thinking of a character who was a master of disguise, of coincidence, this name with its suggestion of inner and outer came to my mind." Both the "rind" and the "heart," Ellison often repeated when describing the symbolic resonance of Rinehart's peculiar name.[8]

Ellison would endow his character Rinehart with additional names that reinforced this sense of mystery. Bliss, as John Callahan notes about Bliss from the second novel, is a name with "contradictory suggestions of states of ignorance and spiritual serenity"; and Proteus is a name for change, for transformation. Ellison would reflect on this name in his Opus II notebook, though it is uncertain whether he had *Invisible Man*'s Rinehart or the second novel's Bliss in mind. "Proteus," he offers by way of definition,

> a prophet sea god in service of Poseidon (Neptune).
> When seized, he would assume different shapes, so
> as to escape prophesying.
>
> Proteus stands for change, illusion, enigma.

This definition squares well with the one he would provide for Rinehart in "Change the Joke and Slip the Yoke." "He is also intended to represent America and change," Ellison explains.

"He has lived so long with chaos that he knows how to ma-nipulate it. . . . He is a figure in a country with no solid past or stable class lines; therefore he is able to move about easily from one to another." After stumbling into a disguise that gives the impression that he is this man named Rinehart, Invisible Man marvels at the range of this stranger's identity. "Still, could he be all of them: Rine the runner and Rine the gambler and Rine the briber and Rine the lover and Rinehart the Reverend? Could he himself be both rind and heart?" For Invisible Man, accepting his invisibility means being willing to explore it, both rind and heart.[9]

As suits such a character, Rinehart would go by many names, and just as many spellings, in Ellison's fiction. In the notes and typescripts for *Invisible Man,* Ellison frequently spells the name "Rhinehart" or "Rhineheart," though it appears in the published novel as "Rinehart." In "Change the Joke and Slip the Yoke," he reverts to the earlier spelling of "Rhinehart," the same he would use in his Opus II notebook. Curiously, the name "Rhinehart" (or "Rinehart," for that matter) does not ap-pear in Ellison's second novel manuscripts. Although the char-acter he describes in the Opus II notebook is undeniably Bliss, Ellison seems to have consciously obscured this lineage. With the name Rinehart missing from the manuscripts, the character Ellison would compose and the one that he conceived in the 1950s are connected in name by "Bliss" alone.[10]

In one of Invisible Man's encounters while wearing the impro-vised disguise of Rinehart, he comes across a strikingly beau-tiful young woman. Though it pains him to deny her, he insists that, despite appearances, he is not the man she seeks. "But Bliss, daddy—Rinehart! You're not trying to put your baby down—Daddy, what did I do?" Only after this plaintive attempt to get him to acknowledge her does she finally recognize him for an imposter. It is an admittedly small moment surrounded by far more dramatic events, and yet in light of Ellison's second novel, it bears tremendous significance. This is the only textual reference to Rinehart's other name in *Invisible Man*.[11]

Bliss, and through Bliss, Rinehart, is the tie that binds Ellison's two novels. In both, Rinehart is indispensable, though his role in the present action of the narrative is limited or, as is the case in *Invisible Man,* nonexistent. Rinehart pushes Invisible Man to conscious awareness of his invisibility, a purpose served in earlier drafts by Leroy's journal, an expurgated portion of the manuscripts that I discuss in the final chapter. Understanding the true nature of possibility, the capacity to exploit experience rather than simply to be subject to it, Invisible Man conceives a plan to put in action his grandfather's deathbed advice. As he conceives it, "Rinehartism" means exploiting people and circumstances from within, "agree[ing] them to death and destruction." This epiphany, however, is short-lived, for it runs him head on into the limitations of such covert action, the impossibility of envisioning a "next step" that satisfies his own sense of social responsibility. The epilogue asserts a tempered faith in democratic possibility while repudiating the cynicism that accompanies covert action even for benevolent aims. Like so many of the other "-isms" the novel proposes and rejects, Rinehartism is fatally limited by its narrow conception of human experience. The inescapable alternative Invisible Man reaches at the novel's end lies in accepting the uncertain possibility of democracy, the philosophy of "speaking for you."

Still, Rinehart haunts *Invisible Man.* Though he appears in the narrative only in the mistaken perception of those who see him in Invisible Man's disguise, he is among the novel's most memorable characters. Certainly Ellison regarded him as such. He described him at length, and with considerable admiration, in an essay published several years after *Invisible Man*.

> He is a cunning man who wins the admiration of those who admire skullduggery and know-how; an American virtuoso of identity who thrives on chaos and swift change; he is greedy, in that his masquerade is motivated by money as well as by the sheer bliss of impersonation; he is godlike, in that he brings new techniques—electric guitars, etc.—to the service of God, and in that there are many men in his image while he is himself unseen; he is a bringer of manna and a worker of miracles, in that he transforms (for winners, of course) pennies into dollars, and thus he feed (and feeds on) the poor. Indeed, one could extend this list in the manner of much myth-mongering criticism until the fiction dissolved into anthropology, but Rhinehart's role in the formal structure of the narrative is to suggest to the hero a mode of escape from Ras, and a means of applying, in yet another form, his grandfather's cryptic advice to his own situation.

As an "American virtuoso of identity who thrives on chaos and swift change," Rinehart is an ur-type in Ellisonian lore. Like the "man of parts" Ellison describes in "The Little Man at Chehaw Station" whose "clashing of styles . . . sound[s] an integrative, vernacular note, an American compulsion to improvise upon the given," Rinehart is a quintessentially American figure. Ellison's unending fascination with this American type, and with the particular manifestation of the type he had

begun but had not finished developing in *Invisible Man*, helps
to explain why he would carry the name, and perhaps more,
into his second novel.[12]

When seen from the perspective of the forty-year compositional history that would follow, Ellison's Opus II notebook in-
habits an unmistakable middle ground between *Invisible Man*
and his manuscript in progress with Rinehart marking the
point of confluence. The "Rinehart" that appears in the notebooks is neither the Rinehart of *Invisible Man* nor Bliss/
Sunraider of the second novel, and yet both. He bears the same
full name as Rinehart from *Invisible Man* and shares with that
character a knack for exploiting and creating chaos. At the
same time, he anticipates Bliss/Sunraider in the rudiments of
his biography. He is of indeterminate race, here specified as
"Negro, white, and Indian"; he is raised in the church by a
black preacher; he runs away and reemerges as a movie man
looking to exploit a small Oklahoma town; he fathers a son
named Severen (though Ellison seems not to have decided for
certain that Severen would be Sunraider's assassin at this point
in the composition); and he gains political office, serving in
the United States Senate, where he is assassinated.

The Opus II notebook makes two clear contributions to
our understanding of the second novel. First, it asserts that
in its earliest conception Ellison imagined the novel around
Rinehart, his name for the boy-preacher turned senator who
would soon bear the names Bliss and Sunraider. Second, it
demonstrates in its connections and disconnections with the
manuscripts to follow certain essential qualities of Ellison's
compositional habits. Which threads did he pick up and which
did he discard? How did his fiction evolve from these fragments of his imagination? The notebook offers a way of read-

ing back through the thousands of pages and decades of distance to the core conception of Ellison's fiction.

Unlike *Invisible Man*'s Rinehart, whose rootlessness is
the form of his freedom, the Opus II Rhinehart is a victim of
his own free will. As Ellison builds his character through the
notebooks, Rhinehart emerges as an individual particularly
trapped by his racial indeterminacy, his protean ability to shift
shades as well as shapes. "The problem of color is there as psychological self-rejection," Ellison writes, "as reason for ques-
tioning, as main source of his sense of rootlessness." Although
Ellison would abandon certain particulars of the character described in the notebooks, this essential quality would remain
as Bliss/Sunraider's central motivation. "He cannot accept his
Negro identity except as something to exploit," Ellison writes,
in a line whose directness belies the complex exercise of this
simple truth in his fiction. Through all the changes Ellison
would put the manuscript through in the years to come, he
held fast to his desire to write "a novel about the rootless
American types who are products of our lon[e]liness."[13]

The novel's central action, as Ellison conceives it in this
embryonic form, concerns Rhinehart's attempt to return to his
neglected past, to embrace his blackness by reconciling with
Hickman, the black man who raised him. The narrative tension would lie in finding out if he could do this in time
or whether his past would catch up to him to cut his life short.
The notebook shows Ellison working through these possibilities. "Integration must come into it," he writes. "Perhaps
Rhinehart is preparing to return to Negro identity when he is
killed. . . . Possibility of a creative relationship between himself
and others, white and black." Within this provisional assertion
one hears echoes of Ellison's more emphatic advocacy of an integrationist ideal, the promise of a fully realized multiracial

democracy. "Must be a 'discovery of America,'" he writes a few pages later. Even here one senses Ellison laying the foundations for a grand Americanist statement in his fiction, one that would pick up where *Invisible Man* left off.

Ellison was still developing this central tension of his fiction, his protagonist's rejection and reconciliation with his racial past, when he wrote the following undated note. One can see Ellison amplifying the murmurs of fictive action from the Opus II notebook, building them toward a narrative crescendo that would express itself in Hickman and Sunraider's hospital bed reconciliation.

> Bliss realizes political and social weakness of Hickman and other Negroes when he's taken from his coffin. . . . But he goes seeking for life among whites, using the agency of racism to punish Negroes for being weak, and to achieve power of his own. As with many politicians politics is a drama in which he plays a role that doesn't necessarily jibe with his own feelings. Nevertheless he feels humiliated by a fate that threw him among Negroes and deprived him of the satisfaction of knowing whether he is a Negro by blood or only by culture and upbringing. He tells himself that he hates Negroes but can't deny his love for Hickman. Resents this too.
>
> He is an [sic] man who sees the weakness in the way societal hierarcy [sic] has delt [sic] with race and it is through the chink that he enters white society and exploits it.

Within this passage are shades of Ellison's high regard for the "virtuoso of identity" that was Rinehart, expressed in his acknowledgment of Bliss's ingenuity in finding his way into white society through a "chink" in the social hierarchy. But that celebration is tempered with bitterness, self-hate, and shame. Rinehart seems to live free of any of these emotions, while Bliss is finally undone by them. This disparity is, perhaps, where Rinehart ends and Bliss begins.[14]

Ellison's notes on the second novel are a record of such evolving forms. Partial tables of contents abound, recasting in subtle—but sometimes dramatic—ways the shape of his fiction. The novel's form would become a source of public speculation as well, both before and after Ellison's death. One storyline that would emerge over the novel's composition was that Ellison was writing not one novel but three. Although Ellison explicitly rejects this on several occasions, he also fuels it with certain provocative statements about the novel's potential structure. The Opus II notebook shows that Ellison was at least considering a tripartite structure: "The first book is that of the frontier. The middle book that of the city. The third book that of the nation." Whether this would mean three separate novels is unclear. Certainly something of this structure remains in Ellison's computer sequences where he has Hickman move from Georgia to Oklahoma to Washington, D.C., the frontier to the seat of national power. The notebook also shows him mapping the rudiments of the plot onto his favored Burkean three-part tragic progression, with "purpose" including Rhinehart's Oklahoma boyhood with Janey as his surrogate mother and Cliofus as his surrogate brother, and his (or Severen's?) time in World War II France and England; "passion" including his return to Oklahoma as the movie man and his encounter with Love New, the half-black, half-Indian shaman; and "perception" including his emergence years later in Washington, D.C.

as a senator, leading to his assassination and, perhaps, the novel's return to Oklahoma to piece together the past after his death. All of these elements are played out in one form or another in Books I and II or the computer sequences, or both.[16]

The notebook also contains details that Ellison seems to have discarded. This includes the thought that Love New might be Rhinehart/Bliss's father. Nothing is done in the second novel with the provocative suggestion that Rhinehart might go to New York City to establish a church, though this seems to pick up on a passage from *Invisible Man* in which Ellison's protagonist, bearing the guise of Rinehart, encounters one of the parishioners of Rinehart's storefront church who recalls having seen him as a boy evangelist down South. Nothing is done with the curious suggestion that the Senator might be assassinated by Puerto Rican terrorists, an echo of the real-life assassination attempt in 1950 on President Harry S. Truman by two Puerto Rican nationalists. Even though the notebook contains a remarkable amount of material that would prove invaluable to the novel in progress as it developed over the years, it was nonetheless a provisional document, full of stops and starts, fits of sudden inspiration and flights of fancy, some of which Ellison seems to reject even as they hit the page.

Rhinehart died in the Opus II notebooks, or at least that is how it seems. The name does not appear in any of the typescripts or the computer sequences. It would be easy enough to assume, then, that Ellison had relinquished the name altogether. Perhaps he considered it too closely associated with *Invisible Man* to function well in a new work of fiction. Perhaps he felt the other names he had came closer to achieving his purpose.

Few things are ever so simple in Ellison's fiction. Though the name Rinehart would disappear from the second novel, the essence of the character would not. Bliss embodies this same radical transformative capacity. Indeed, at the very moment of Bliss's birth, Rinehart appears, embedded in Hickman's description of Bliss's mother just moments before she gives birth. "A pair of purple smears sagging shuteyed in my hands and me standing there holding her unable to let her fall—if we ever learn to feel real revulsion of the flesh—any flesh—that's when hell will truly erupt down here and the whole unhappy history become an insane waste; if we ever learn to hate the mere rind in the same way we ignore the spirit and the heart and the hopeful possibility underneath."[16]

Rinehart made his final appearance in an unlikely place, on a computer floppy disk. Among the hundreds of files saved to Ellison's computers is one labeled "Rhinehart." Although its precise date is lost, it appears to have been created in the mid-1980s, likely in 1986. The file is not a part of the computer sequences of narrative, but instead a note concerning certain plot details in the novel. It reads as if it could have come from Ellison's 1950s notebook, though it dates from thirty-five years later. I've included it below in its entirety:

> Rhineheart has contemplated suicide, but rejects it out of a desire to curse God for placing him in an ambiguous position. Thus he decides to recreate himself in his own uncertain image. All of his mythomania springs from that *conscious* decision. It is this which links up psychologically with his *American* rootlessness and ironic self-rejection—even after he has become a U.S. senator, and motivates much of his strange behavior. He is a *superman* who has rejected the pose. He lives in that nebulous area between illusion and reality. Rhine and heart, yes, but

> really he has rejected his human center, and that
> center is located in his cultural background as a
> Negro.

As before, Ellison emphasizes Rhineheart's ambiguity, his capacity for self-transformation, and his quintessentially American condition of rootlessness. Inhabiting "that nebulous area between illusion and reality," he remains largely unchanged in spirit from *Invisible Man*'s master of chaos. "Rhine and heart, yes," he concludes, reiterating his favorite symbolic meaning, "but really he has rejected his human center, and that center is located in his cultural background as a Negro." It is in these last crucial phrases that Ellison endows this Rhineheart, whom he would call Bliss whom he would call Sunraider, with significance neither the Rinehart of *Invisible Man* nor even the Rhinehart of his notebook could bear. The dichotomy embodied in Bliss/Sunraider is Ellison's evocation of that process of acceptance and rejection. In this process, an intermediary identity like Rhinehart has no clear place.[17]

Perhaps in those thirty-five years separating this note from his first Ellison had discovered that the character he called Rhinehart could really exist only at these two extremes: Bliss and Sunraider. Though he could call him Rhinehart outside the narrative, he would not use the name within. Here was a character whose central dilemma was finding a way back to his past, to his Bliss, from a present lifetimes removed.[18]

Tracing the textual history of an invisible character like Rinehart offers an opportunity for imaginative projection into the characters of Ellison's second novel, a way of considering the tough decisions Ellison undoubtedly would have had to make if he ever wished to publish the book. The appearance and disappearance of key characters throughout the process of composition calls attention to just how unfinished the second novel truly is. In addition to the fact that it lacks *Invisible Man*'s seamless narrative structure, which takes its reader from beginning to middle to end, it also lacks the firm editorial hand that would have shaped the mass of manuscripts into a coherent whole. To put it another way, for Ellison to have finished his novel, he would have had to engage in a process of addition—writing the transitions to supply the necessary connective tissue between episodes—but also of subtraction—making the tough decisions about character and scene that would have fashioned an aesthetic whole.

Ellison's second novel is teeming with characters, even a surplus of voices. He gives life to so many that the putative protagonist—be it, at any given time in composition of the manuscript, Hickman or Sunraider or McIntyre—must often compete for control of the narrative. Occasionally, Ellison even drafts the same scene from multiple perspectives. He worries his notes with whether to have this or that character take a particular action. He muses on the possible relationships he might forge among his disparate cast of characters. The result is a living community of voices, animated in ways that might not even be sustainable in a unified work of fiction. Perhaps such polyphony can thrive only in the vast, ungoverned space sanctioned by the novel's incompletion.

The best testament to the second novel's power of polyphony is the character of Severen, Rhinehart/Bliss/Sunraider's estranged son and eventual assassin. Severen's name appears in the Opus II notebook, where Ellison muses upon the psychological implications of patricide. Like his father, Severen appears white but is culturally black, having been raised by Janey Glover, Alonzo Hickman's former sweetheart. Ellison's early notes reveal that he conceived the novel at least in part as Severen's story of race, culture, and redemption. He is both the agent of the novel's central action, the assassination, as well as an interpreter of experience. Ellison often reminds himself that the reader must hear Severen's voice. In a vivid passage from some of his early notes for the novel, Ellison channels that voice:

> You know of my father Senator Bliss P. Rhineheart because of his activities in the Senate and later because (he was shot down) of what happened to him on the senate floor, but you ~~wouldn't~~ are probably surprised to hear that he has a son, and more surprising of all that he had a son like me. Of course, he was a hero, and to some at least a beloved man, a statesman, and you knew him. But I—well, I don't think you know me any better than I knew him. Nor do you care to know me, for I trail with me unpleasant odors of slavery, civil war, and internal strife; old angers, unresolved conflicts; gnawing, semi-conscious motives; dark possibilities; anti-Puritan potentialities, even visions of hell fire. And yet I am my father's son. He didn't deny me but he didn't acknowledge me either. I could not say to him, "Why hast thou forsaken me?" because he made no commitment to me. He was gone before I arrived and the message went astray, the wireless garbled the text, and beside[s], he had even then gone on to another country, city, state.

Ellison would retain the redolent New Testament quotation from this passage as he composed his novel: "Why hast thou forsaken me?" For Severen, it is an unrequited query, a question he wonders whether he even has the right to ask. For Sunraider, however, it will become a marker of a hidden past. This will be both the phrase that cues the young Bliss to rise from the coffin during Hickman's theatrical tent revival services and the words Sunraider cries out after being shot. It becomes a recurring motif in a novel that, at its core, centers upon fathers and sons. The retention of this small detail, essential to the novel as Ellison would imagine it in the decades to come, is a testament to just how much Ellison already knew about his book, even before he had really begun to write.[19]

It is no idle critical conjecture to say that Ellison had *Invisible Man* in mind when conceiving Severen's role in the second novel. Ellison's working notes show him drawing closely on the former novel's organizational structure in plotting his new manuscript. One note whose manual typeface suggests that Ellison composed it before he started using an IBM Selectric in the early 1960s bears two columns of text. On the left, Ellison has recorded *Invisible Man*'s major episodes using single words or short phrases and mapping it onto a Burkean tragic structure. On the right, he has written a provisional sequence for the second novel. Several things he mentions in the outline are not clearly reflected in the manuscripts, including the initial incident of the "shooting along road in the dark." Perhaps most striking of all for those familiar with the published portions of Ellison's second novel, including all the excerpts Ellison himself would publish, along with both *Juneteenth* and *Three Days Before the Shooting . . .* , is the central role Ellison imagines for Severen. "Severen is hero," he writes, "and already worthy of sacrifice but this must not be lost sight of in development." Reading through the typescripts, where Severen is a shadowy figure at best, and certainly through the computer drafts, where he is all but invisible, it is hard to imagine him in this heroic posture.[20]

If Severen was so critical to the plot, then why did Ellison find it so challenging to integrate him into the polyphonic structure of the novel? Severen is a shadowy figure in the 1970s typescripts, and hardly a presence at all in the computer files. The computer files seem to suggest that Hickman arrives in Oklahoma not long after Severen's departure—or perhaps with a fortuitous overlap (in some drafts he suggests that Hickman, in fact, leads Severen to his target). The textual evidence of Ellison's struggle with Severen is apparent throughout the manuscripts.

For all of his importance, however, Severen gradually loses his corporeal presence in the novel, becoming—like his father, Sunraider—a disembodied voice, a shadow, a name and abstract motive, and finally almost nothing at all. At times Hickman wonders whether he has seen him in a crowd, but by the time he looks back to confirm it, Severen is gone. The closest we come to him is in Book I of the typescripts when McIntyre recalls a wartime encounter with a soldier and conspirator with the French resistance named Severen. But even in this memory, Severen hardly speaks. Later, McIntyre visits the morgue after the shooting to see Severen's corpse. It is the clearest description we ever get of him. What must have evolved in Ellison's conception of the novel that a character he once considered for the protagonist would end up becoming something closer to a literary conceit? And what vestiges of Severen remain in the novel's shape as Ellison revised, then revised again, always approaching but never reaching publication? By the time Ellison shifted his composition of the novel to the computer, Severen was someone talked about but never talking, someone who may or may not be visible.

Severen's evolving place in the second novel—first a central figure, then reduced to a conceit—is not without precedent in Ellison's fiction. *Invisible Man*, too, is shaped by the absence of several strong characters brought vividly to life in the expurgated drafts. Together, these characters tell a shadow history of Ellison's fiction; they are his true invisible men—and women.

V
1950

Invisible Man once had a wife. As hard as it is to believe of a novel so thoroughly bereft of eros, in which the few romantic or sexual encounters that do occur quickly become occasions for anger or laughter or both, Ellison toyed with the idea of his nameless protagonist marrying a white member of the Brotherhood, a woman named Louise. In the working notes for the novel Ellison writes the following by way of explaining the relationship:

> Louise is the one person in the organization ~~that~~ whom he can believe accepts him as a human being and not as a thing to be manipulated for abstract political purposes. She stands as a vessel of democracy and freedom and fertility which he can win only by accepting the [task of] defining himself against the concrete nature of his world. ~~He married Louise~~ but is never quite sure whether it is because she is white or because he actually loves her. Her whiteness is a problem to him. He is proud of

it and he hates it. . . . Louise is the one person in organization who accepts him as a human being and not as something to be manipulated for abstract political purposes. She might be called a vessel of democracy or freedom ~~fertility~~, whom he can win only by accepting his own humanity. He, however, is so divided against himself that he cannot accept her, cannot believe that she loves him and in the end betrays her; not because she is untrue or has denied his humanity but because he rebels against his sense of self . . . must come to him through a white woman, because he can never feel sure that she could love him.[1]

Ellison may have crossed out the mention of Invisible Man's marriage to Louise in this note, but the significance of the relationship remains. As Ellison imagined it, *Invisible Man* would be a kind of love story, albeit one in which the primary motive of the relationship was not the communion of souls but the fashioning of an individual identity. This textual note and the manuscript drafts that reflect the spirit of it in fiction suggest a radical departure from the published novel, a new fictive vision in which Invisible Man's relationship with a woman is not only significant but elemental.

Of course, as this passage attests, the love Ellison describes is hardly a healthy and balanced one. Love for Invisible Man is about self-definition, not human connection. Louise is a "vessel of democracy and freedom and fertility," not a fully articulated character with her own motives and capacities. She is conceived, in other words, as all the other characters are in *Invisible Man*, as a foil against which Ellison might reveal certain facets of his nameless protagonist's evolving character. Ellison's decision to restrict the role of Louise, as well as that of other female characters, went hand in hand with his broader decision to limit the role of love and sex in the novel, which, in turn, seems to have resulted from his awareness that he was better able to render his character's search for identity without the complications that love presented.

Three years after *Invisible Man*'s publication, Ellison sat for a long interview with the *Paris Review* concerning all manner of the novel's themes and his own methods of composition. Here he makes the case, if not quite convincingly, that the Brotherhood is not a reference to the Communist Party; he also asserts that the epilogue is a "necessary statement," not a tacked on addition to the narrative; and he explains in clear terms why Invisible Man never found love. "Look," he says in exasperation, "didn't you find the book at all *funny*? I felt that such a man as this character would have been incapable of a love affair; it would have been inconsistent with his personality." It is, indeed, difficult to imagine Invisible Man relating to another character on such intimate terms. As other critics have noted, Ellison makes allusions to his protagonist's potency (the inference left to hang in the air with Invisible Man's late-night walks from the girls' dormitory in the early campus scenes, or the dalliance with the plump and nameless wife of one of the Brotherhood's operatives). The most memorable moment when Invisible Man is forced into physical proximity with a woman is, of course, when Sybil begs for him to "rape" her, to be the black buck in her perverse fantasy. That he demurs in favor of writing in lipstick across her pale stomach that she has been raped by Santa Claus is perhaps less a statement on his virility than it is on his dawning awareness of the necessity of directed action. It is, after all, in the hours after his encounter with Sybil that Invisible Man confronts Ras the Destroyer, endures the chaos of the riot, and evades his captors before slipping into his underground retreat.

The single-mindedness of this personal narrative, the protagonist's journey from ignorance to awareness to the verge of action, is necessarily an isolated one. Ellison's process of revision is best summed up as a process of stripping away the integuments encasing this central action, the characters and scenes, many of which are crackling with fictive energy, that ultimately distract from his novel's necessary momentum. This explains the erasure of Leroy, a naked plot devise and thematic crutch that ended up taking away from the development of the protagonist. It also might help explain the indefinite image of Rinehart, a character so charismatic that even his shadowed presence threatens to envelop Invisible Man as the novel nears its conclusion.

But of all the cuts Ellison made in the name of unifying his novel around his central character's struggle, none are more palpable in their absence than the erasure or foreshortening of his female characters. The existence of Louise and another of Invisible Man's lovers, a young black woman named Cleo, a fellow boarder at Mary Rambo's house, in the drafts of the novel combined with their absence in the published text suggest a provocative and, at times, puzzling textual history for one of the twentieth century's most emphatic literary assertions of individual identity. Early drafts of the novel suggest not only a prominent role for these women but the essential function of Invisible Man's relationships with them in Ellison's rendering of his protagonist's emerging identity. They are, in other words, amanuenses as well as characters in their own right.

Reading Louise, Cleo, and the other invisible women of the working drafts back into *Invisible Man* offers a rare opportunity to reconsider the novel by filling in, if imperfectly and provisionally, its most glaring deficiencies, including the absence of fully rendered female characters and the limitations on love that the novel sets for itself. How does Invisible Man's quest for identity change when it is mediated at least in part through his love affair with Louise, a white woman, and with Cleo, a black woman? Does reading these women back into the novel redress critical grievances, complicate them, or even exacerbate them? And how do Louise and Cleo, both their presence in the drafts and their absence in the published novel, shed light on the love relationships in Ellison's second novel— McIntyre's interracial romance with Laura, Bliss/Sunraider's protracted dalliance with Lavatrice, and Hickman's star-crossed love affair with Janey? What emerges is a story of Ellison's own process of artistic maturation, the expansion of his expressive capacity as a writer of fiction to render emotions unexplored in *Invisible Man*.

As early as the 1970s, when drafts of *Invisible Man* still remained locked away in Ellison's personal files, critics like Claudia Tate had already begun recuperating the "invisible women" in Ellison's novel, arguing that they, "like the underground station masters of the American slave era, . . . assist the Invisible Man along his course to freedom." According to Tate, characters like Mary; the "magnificent blonde" from the Battle Royal; the Brotherhood operative, Emma; the unnamed wife of a party leader; and Sybil, the wife of another leader, combine to "embody the knowledge he needs to stage his escape." The culmination of this process, his move from underground to aboveground, is forever suspended, Tate argues, because the novel lacks a female character in the conclusion to help Invisible Man see his way through. Such a reading, though schematic, usefully recenters the novel around its female characters or, more precisely, around Invisible Man's relationships, romantic and otherwise, with these women.[3]

Tate's argument proves prescient when one considers the considerable role female characters play in the drafts of the novel, material Tate could not have consulted when writing her essay. She did, however, have access to the small portion of the drafts that Ellison published in 1963 as "Out of the Hospital and Under the Bar," on which she draws heavily to make her case for the importance of Mary Rambo. The full drafts of *Invisible Man* were made available to scholars after Ellison's death, and a handful of critics have since taken up Tate's call, responding with a range of critical explications of the novel's female characters. Barbara Foley, for instance, reads Ellison's erasure of Louise as the central part of his effacement of his communist sympathies. Rather than a question of gender, in other words, Louise's erasure was primarily a matter of politics. By comparison, James Smethurst reads the elimination of characters like Louise and the limitation of others like Mary as consistent with Ellison's emerging vision of rendering his protagonist's "triumphant heroic individualism." He ties this aesthetic effort to a political one of contributing to "the powerful engagement with the ideological underpinning of the Cold War and the American Century." Lena Hill reads Ellison's decision to limit his female characters as a conscious redirection of intention. "While the drafts dramatize the stereotype of black men's desire for white women," she argues, "the finished text stresses the social parallel between white women and black men." These divergent critical interpretations suggest something of the indeterminacy of the drafts as they relate to Ellison's evolving vision of his female characters.[4]

The range of critical explorations of female characters in

the drafts of *Invisible Man* highlight vital questions for understanding Ellison's compositional process and thematic range. Although most agree that Ellison foreshortened his female characters during the process of revision from the drafts to the published novel, a wide critical distance separates the interpretations of Ellison's motive. Did Ellison restrict the role of his women as a means to open up avenues of empathy between his protagonist's struggle to assert his independent identity over and against racial stereotype and the parallel struggle of women to assert their own visibility? Or was it, instead, a signal that, for all the liberating force behind his protagonist's racial struggle, Ellison himself was unable to get beyond his own hegemonic tendencies when it came to gender? If the latter is the case, then it is as much a failure of craft as it is of politics, a sign of Ellison's inability to see the other in the self, the very challenge his protagonist sets for readers in the final lines of the novel—the task of speaking for you. The former, however, is more intriguing because it respects the fact that Ellison's drafts reveal an acute interest in his female characters and their interactions with his protagonist.

Ellison's drafts at times offer psychologically complex depictions of male-female relationships, ones that allow for more nuanced renderings of romantic love and sex than the unrealistic, near-comic encounters in the published novel. Of course, *Invisible Man* as it would be published in 1952 is anything but a love story. One consequence of its dogged focus on an individual man's search for identity is that all other characters, including all female characters, often end up looking foreshortened and schematic. Reading the novel in progress, however, expands the interpretive range of Ellison's effort, revealing the novel as originally conceived (and reconceived numerous times) in the drafts as a palimpsest, showing underneath the published novel. By looking closely at the decisions Ellison made regarding his female characters and their relationship to his protagonist, we stand to gain as much from what he leaves out as from what he puts in.

Early in the prologue, Invisible Man recalls the time "when [he] was trying to escape in the night from Ras the Destroyer. But that's getting too far ahead of the story, almost to the end, although the end was in the beginning and lies far ahead." This critical passage makes allusive reference to one of the central ideological battles of the novel, the chaos and conflagration of the riot, and Invisible Man's assertion of his beliefs in the face of Ras's exhortations. It also underscores the boomeranging structure of the novel, a narrative that doubles back on itself quite literally through the prologue and epilogue as well as through the range of themes that express themselves through Ellison's method of repetition with a difference.[5]

In the published novel, Invisible Man discovers his basement hideaway while fleeing from Ras the Destroyer. The drafts, however, reveal one of the most dramatic textual emendations in all the manuscripts: a one-for-one substitution of Louise for Ras the Destroyer. As originally conceived, the passage read: "when I was trying to escape in the night from Louise, Louise, Louise—now that was a woman of women! But that's getting too far ahead of the story, almost to the end, although the end was in the beginning and lies far ahead." The simple transfer of a name, the work of a few strokes of the pen, would forever shift the direction of the manuscript. Rather than running from love, Invisible Man runs from death itself. Rather than extolling the virtues of a romantic paragon, he calls attention to the destructive capacity of his principle adversary. Seldom can a single textual change, one that retains the syntactical structure of the sentence no less, have such striking implications. More than a love story, more even than a character is lost with the disappearance Louise. In her absence, Ellison had to reconceive certain basic facets of his narrative; his protagonist's motive, his dramatic tone, even the substance of his political message, all had to shift to account for her absence.[6]

Ellison's change puts in mind a critical insight offered more than thirty years ago by the critic Marilyn Nelson Waniek. In her 1975 essay "The Space Where Sex Should Be: Toward a Definition of the Black American Literary Tradition," Waniek makes the claim that certain African-American male authors, Ellison among them, often put racial conflict in the place where sex and romantic love should be in their fiction. "In the space where sex should be is instead the awful confrontation of Black self with white self, and the Black self with white society," she writes. She cites works by writers such as Richard Wright and James Baldwin. Indeed, it was Baldwin who first phrased such a critique when he observed in his 1961 reflection on Richard Wright, "Alas, Poor Richard," that "in most of the novels written by Negroes until today ... there is a great space where sex ought to be; and what usually fills this space is violence." Waniek builds on Baldwin's insight, pointing to Ellison's *Invisible Man,* which she describes as a novel uniquely fixated on the struggles of a young black male protagonist in almost perfect isolation from women, love, and sex. Ellison's substitution of Ras for Louise is a remarkable literalization of what both Baldwin and Waniek theorized, a conscious decision to disencumber his protagonist from the complications of love and sex and, with them, of his female character.[7]

Reading Ellison's notes and riffs effectively brings Louise back to life. In a passage that shares its tone of reverie with the

excised passage from the prologue, Ellison offers a nuanced description of Louise and her relation to his nameless protagonist:

> And I knew at that moment that it was not her
> color, but the voice and if there was anything in the
> organization to which I could give myself com-
> pletely, it was she. If I could work with her, be al-
> ways near her, then I could have all that the Trustees
> had promised and failed to give and more. And if
> she was not the meaning of the struggle for the oth-
> ers, for me she would be the supremest prize of all.
> 'Oh you fair warrior,' my mind raced on, 'You dear,
> sweet, lovely thing, for you I'd rock the nation with
> a word. You'll be my Liberty and Democracy, Hope
> and Truth and Beauty, the justification for man-
> hood, the motive for courage and cunning; for you
> I'll make myself into this new name they've given
> me and I'll believe that Brother Jack and the others
> mean what they say about creating a world in which
> even men like me can be free.' . . . I took a drink and
> for an instant I remembered the Vet laughing in the
> bus as it shot away from the campus. . . . So I would
> *play* the fool, and if it was my being black that made
> me desire the white meat of the chicken, then I'd
> accept my desire along with the chitterlings and
> sweet potato pie.[8]

Like the passage from the prologue where Louise becomes Ras, Ellison renders Invisible Man's voice in ecstatic
tones, intoxicated by its own rhetoric, suggesting a narrator
lost in love, or perhaps even driven by obsession. Louise, this
passage suggests, is Invisible Man's means of entry into the

Brotherhood, but also the origin of a good part of his new identity. She is both the source of his racial conflictedness and the means of his self-expression. How, then, could a novel that began at least in part as an interracial love story end up as a self-consciously masculine struggle for self-assertion and identity?

The moment Ellison excludes romantic love from his novel is the moment *Invisible Man* becomes a classic, because it is the moment in which Ellison truly begins the challenging work of having his protagonist search for a reason for being and an identity independent of personal relationships, romantic or otherwise. The identity that takes shape through Invisible Man's telling of the story of his own invisibility and reaches its final form in the epilogue is a species of democratic individualism that is at once sui generis and yet caught up in an inescapable network of democratic mutuality. Our fate is to become one out of many, Invisible Man writes, echoing the national motto. Invisible Man's fate, rendered emphatically in the novel's closing line, is to be both individual and representative man.

Louise, it seems, was finally less a character than a shortcut for Ellison, a way of writing around the difficult challenge his fiction presented to him. Instead of rendering a love relationship in full, he resorts to emotional shorthand. Romantic commonplaces and rhetorical extravagances ("shock the world with a word") take the place of a more organic explication of motive. Getting his readers to believe that his protagonist will do something, anything, for love or infatuation is not much of a literary challenge, either to the writer or to the reader. It relies almost exclusively on stock emotion and easy assumptions of what a character in love will do. In so many of the passages from the drafts that involve Louise, Invisible Man is a fool for love, and acknowledgedly so—"So I would *play* the fool," he says, accepting his every desire, though it be a tired cliché.

The best writing about love and romance finds a way to start with the stereotype, admit its truth, and then write its way toward the human center that such banalities obscure. Ellison, certainly at this stage in his literary career, does not appear up to the task of handling romantic love relationships in fiction. So by eliminating love as a motive entirely from his fiction, he forces himself to substitute in its place some other, more tangible motive. This brings Ellison back to what for him at least is a more comprehensible and organic subject of fiction: the quest for, and assertion of, an individual identity within a collective context.

The early drafts are evidence to the fact that for a time Ellison imagined Invisible Man's relationship with Louise as one of the primary grounds on which his dawning awareness would show itself. His identity would largely vitiate itself in their relationship. Ellison's working notes provide a compelling account of Louise's centrality, worth quoting at length.

> He [Invisible Man] becomes so insecure that he is never at peace unless he is treated as an inferior. Thus in a democratic organization he feels at peace only when the patterns of American race etiquette are suddenly observed. Yet, he is aware of his own sensitivity and intelligence and resents the power of his white colleagues over him.
>
> In this state he meets Louise, a young woman of great charm. Louise is the one person in the organization whom he can believe accepts him as a human being. He regards her as a symbol of de-

mocracy, of freedom and fertility which he can win only by accepting the task of defining himself against the opposition of the world. However, he is not sure whether he is attracted to Louise for herself or for her whiteness. Her whiteness is quite a problem. He is proud of it and he hates it. He receives pleasure from the resentment of those who object when they walk down the street. He is also afraid of the danger which he feels this involves and insists that she spend long hours beneath the sunlamp baking her complexion painfully close to that of a mulatto. Like Othello, whose situation he now parodies, he cannot accept himself nor believe that anyone like Louise could find him attractive. Finally, to end his conflict he drives her away.[9]

He meets Louise at the height of his aimlessness, and she gives him a means of self-definition. Not only does she "accept him as a human being," but she provides him with a kind of social capital, one invested with great symbolic weight. "He regards her," Ellison writes, "as a symbol of democracy, of freedom and fertility which he can win only by accepting the task of defining himself against the opposition of the world." Even in driving her away, he is taking a final step toward self-definition. How could a character so seemingly central to the exercise of the novel end up disappearing? What is lost, what is sacrificed in Ellison's decision to remove her from the novel? And what do we stand to gain from reading her back into it? The reasons for her erasure seem clear enough: Invisible Man ultimately does seem to be a character ill-suited for love, a necessarily solo figure seeking self-definition. Additionally, the implications of writing a novel in 1952 with an interracial love story at its center must have been clear to Ellison. He may well have considered that his book would have gotten lost in the sensation, dismissed as just another titillating dime-store novel.

This racial argument does not hold true for another major female character that Ellison excised entirely from the manuscript, the young black boarder at Mary's house named Cleo. Invisible Man encounters Cleo when he takes a room at Mary's. Cleo is the former lover of Leroy, a merchant seaman lost at sea, and Invisible Man is taken by her almost immediately. It is Cleo finally who asserts her desires on Invisible Man, though they are unable to consummate the act. In his working notes, Ellison associates Cleo with one of the muses—the muse of history from whom her name is drawn—endowing her as well with a kind of symbolic agency. It is ultimately the idea of Cleo rather than the reality of her that is most compelling to Ellison. In the most explicit sexual encounter in all the drafts of *Invisible Man*—indeed, in all of Ellison's fiction, published or unpublished—he writes of the couple's difficulty in consummating their physical union. As it turns out, Leroy has tried on numerous occasions to take Cleo's virginity, but her hymen has thwarted his efforts. Ellison offers several renditions of the scene, one involving a series of elaborate circumlocutions and extended metaphors of plowing fields, another expressing the circumstances more directly: "Break it, Please break it!" Cleo yells in exasperation at one point. The scene renders sex as a farcical affair. It plays sex for the broadest possible laughs while attempting to stay within sight of the narrative tone. The scene bears out James Smethurst's claim that Ellison extols the sexual agency of his black women characters. "In other words," he continues, "these women demonstrate an open sexual interest in black men—and sometimes a willingness to trade sex for money or other material gains; only they are not interested in *him*." Even, as in the case of Cleo, when the attention is directed at Invisible Man, the result is failure. Although this encounter breaks with what Smethurst characterizes as the published novel's "perverse or mercenary" sexual encounters, it nonetheless underscores the fractured connection between men and women, and specifically between Invisible Man and women, that has come to characterize the novel.[10]

Even in writing this scene, Ellison appears to have had misgivings about the nature of Cleo's characterization. "Perhaps Cleo (or Depphenia) should be a more complicated character," he writes at the top of one draft. "Folk transformed by city, she might foreshadow his political agon." But Ellison would finally find no function for Cleo in the novel. However, her character serves a significant critical purpose in reflecting on the manuscripts. As Michael and Lena Hill note, "Drafts of these scenes trouble a number of critical readings by revealing Ellison's serious contemplation of a sexual relationship between the narrator and a black woman." They associate Cleo's erasure with Ellison's telescoping of all things related to Mary Rambo's boarding house and the Harlem community in general. "In a strange twist that Ellison clearly understood," they speculate, "Mary's reduction produces this dramatic streamlining of the narrator's identity exploration."[11]

It seems that even when Cleo was included in the manuscript, her primary purpose was to underscore Invisible Man's connection to Leroy, who becomes a double in a way. "You and Leroy are just alike," she tells him. "He sure would have been a big man if this hadn't happened." Invisible Man lives in Leroy's room, reads his journal, even wears his underwear, so it stands to reason that he might also have interest in his girlfriend. Ellison conjures Cleo as a kind of rite of passage for his protagonist, using her name as an evocative clue. Clio, the muse of history, was also known as "the proclaimer." She, indeed, serves to chronicle and extol the past of her dead lover, Leroy, even as she challenges Invisible Man to action. In an undated note, Ellison speculates on her function in the lives of both men:

> He [Leroy] is eligible for sacrifice because he could not satisfy Cleo (the sexual offense), because he is too ideal (the offense of the absolute), and because he fails in the interest of intellect to take some crucially necessary action.
>
> He must be built up into real person through conversation of others. For Mary he is potential leader and son, for Cleo a lover, for Treadwell he is a symbol of danger, evil, and intellectual liberation. IVM must sum up LeRoy in his own mind at different stages of his own development.
>
> Cleo must come to his room after scene of picture hanging, an unsuccessful, or only partially successful encounter, after which he dreams of incident translated into handicraft, piecework, equivalents. Following this he goes next day to encounter trustees and receives knowledge of his predicament.[12]

The importance of their sexual encounter remaining unconsummated is critical for Ellison, if only, it seems, because it provides his protagonist with an occasion to aestheticize his experience. It becomes a kind of indefinite motive, encouraging him to pursue his designated course of action.

What, then, do we make of Ellison's decision to remove these two romantic relationships, with Louise and with Cleo, from

Invisible Man? They mirror in some ways Bigger Thomas's dual relationships in Richard Wright's *Native Son.* Of course, the unmistakable difference is that Bigger's relations with women end in two acts of murder: the first after he has an indeterminate encounter with Mary Dalton, the white daughter of his wealthy employer; the second after he rapes his black girlfriend, Bessie. With Mary, Bigger associates social capital as well as a kind of white radicalism that makes him uncomfortable and even resentful. With Bessie, he seems to feel both sexual license and a certain disregard or even contempt for her. His relationships with and violent acts against these women define the novel, setting the terms of Bigger's development. When Bigger finally finds the voice to assert his selfhood in the novel's last scene, he does so by affirming his crime against Mary: "What I killed for must have been good. What I killed for I am." In the very moment in which it would seem the focus is on the singularity of Wright's protagonist, attention turns to his relationship to a woman.[13]

That the drafts of *Invisible Man* seems to echo *Native Son* while the published novel does not speaks to matters both of craft and of theme. Does Ellison's evasion of sex and romance and, with them, of female characters, speak to a deficit of expression? Does it suggest an inherent chauvinism? In other words, do we understand Ellison's actions as personal politics or literary craft—or perhaps a bit of both? One way of addressing these questions is to look, as we have done, to the working drafts and notes that led to *Invisible Man.* Another is to consider all this material, along with the published novel, next to the manuscripts of the second novel, in which a series of relationships between male and female characters suggests the evolution of Ellison's craft, if not also of his thought.

For Ellison in *Invisible Man,* it appears that writing about love meant writing melodrama. Much of the material he removed was simply inconsistent in tone with his more expansive and probing passages that surrounded it. They seem labored and even comical by comparison. By disallowing himself the easy recourse of love as the motive for Invisible Man's actions, Ellison forced his imagination into conceiving alternative understandings of his character's motivations—ones that as a writer he was more suited to describe, given the challenge of writing authentically about love and romance. This makes it all the more striking that Ellison would return to the motive of love in his second novel. This time, however, he appears to have broadened his emotive range. Ellison writes about love and sex in the second novel in a way that it would seem unlikely to expect from the author of a novel as arid in its male-female relations as *Invisible Man*. Each of his primary characters in the second novel is shaped, without being overwhelmed or completely defined, by his romantic relationships with women. In each of these instances, the relationships are relics of the past; the lovers are somehow estranged from one another or otherwise distanced from the immediacy of their emotions. Nonetheless, these relationships undergird the very structure of Ellison's fiction. What emerges is a growing sense of Ellison's development as an author capable of empathetic projections across distance and difference.

Just as Ellison would initially conceive an interracial love affair in *Invisible Man*, he does the same in the second novel. This time, however, the roles are reversed, with a white male protagonist and a black female love interest. Welborn McIntyre, the first-person narrator of Book I, is a white D.C. newspaper reporter whom we first encounter in the Senate visitor's gallery listening to Senator Adam Sunraider deliver what will be his final speech. After the shooting, McIntyre finds himself thrust into the center of the mysterious action, both as a consequence of his reportorial role and, more provocatively, because of a palpable but indefinite personal connection that links him to the dramatic events of the day. As McIntyre waits outside the senator's hospital room for news on his condition, he puzzles over the seemingly irreconcilable connection between Sunraider, an unrepentant racist, and Hickman, an elderly black minister. Despite all common sense, Sunraider has called for Hickman to attend to him at the hospital, and Hickman has willingly obliged. Perhaps in his attempt to comprehend this mysterious interracial connection, McIntyre reflects on his own past love affair with a young black woman in Harlem named Laura.

Like the undeniable allure Invisible Man feels for Louise, McIntyre feels something equally powerful, even magical, in the cross-racial appeal of his relationship with Laura. "Personally, I lived in a state of high delight," he recalls. "I felt that Laura endowed me with a special potency, thus I considered myself the possessor of a mysterious knowledge which gave a touch of swagger whenever we strolled the easily challenged streets arm-in-arm, eye to eye, mentally hypnotized by our daring." Here love is embodied through a kind of silent protest, an outward display of inward affection intended to shock the community into enlightenment. In an undated note from the *Invisible Man* materials, Ellison remarks on this same experience with Invisible Man and Louise, that "he receives pleasure from the resentment of those who object when they walk down the street." In both instances, the display of interracial love is a political act. For McIntyre and Laura, their love affair is "given further sanction by our group zeal to improve, redeem and, if need be, revolutionize society. But basically we were in love, and in our circles it was agreed that Laura and I represented, if not the future, at least a good *earnest* of that time when the old conflicts left unresolved by the great war between the states (and we were nothing if not historically-minded) and the wounds, outrages and inequities which haunted contemporary society would be resolved by transcendent love." This concept of revolution by means of transcendent love is a familiar one in Ellison's fiction, given definition in *Invisible Man,* not simply in the excised relationship between Invisible Man and Louise, but even in the published novel, albeit in abstracted form.[14]

Although eros has little place in the published novel, agape and philia do appear. One of the most emotionally charged sections of *Invisible Man* comes with the death of Tod Clifton and the public mourning that follows. Clifton represents the strength of the community, but also its continued susceptibility to violence. Invisible Man's eulogy, drawn as it is from the energy of the assembled masses, is perhaps the novel's greatest expression of love and human connection. At first the crowd's response, even their very presence at the memorial, confuses Invisible Man. "Why were they here? Why had they found us? Because they knew Clifton? Or for the occasion his death gave them to express their protestations, a time and a place to come together, to stand touching and sweating and breathing and looking in a common direction? Was either explanation adequate in itself? Did it signify love or politicized hate? And could politics ever be an expression of love?"[15]

In these searching questions, Invisible Man is stumbling toward an expression of a kind of political philosophy. As John Callahan has written in reference to this passage:

> Rooted in his own muddled motives, his questions
> nevertheless reach out toward that American and

African-American conviction that an individual's
deepest personal beliefs and experiences are somehow bound up with the political life of the nation.
When he looks out and sees faces in the crowd, Invisible Man realizes that for these people politics is
an expression of love in the complex sense identified elsewhere by Ellison as "that condition of
man's being at home in the world which is called
love and which we term democracy." . . . In this
context Invisible Man seeks fraternity and community, if not democracy. Unexpectedly, he hears the
sudden solo voice of an old man raised in "Many
Thousands Gone" and suddenly understands that
for these people love intensifies the engagement
with the world that becomes inevitably political.[16]

Ellison reprises this philosophy decades later, this time
transposing the source of the love from a communal one to a
romantic one through McIntyre's relationship with Laura.
"'Democracy is love, love is democracy,'" we often said, and
our friends agreed. And this became, for a time, my personal
slogan. Laura was lovely, eager, and brave, and there was much
about the world which she didn't know, and I was delighted
and proud to teach her of the many things which lay beyond
the arbitrary boundaries placed around her freedom, and mine.
We were dedicated to love and society, thus we looked to the
future but, as it turned out, not quite far enough ahead." In the
detritus of the failed relationship, McIntyre sees his own failure—of interracial empathy, of political defiance. Ellison
would also have us see McIntyre's naïveté, his thought that he
could will himself past all social norms simply by the zeal of
his own feeling and his commitment to learning blackness. "I

spent hours in Harlem," he explains. "I visited clubs, attended dances, absorbed the slang, the music, the turns of phrase, made great efforts to identify with all of Laura." We hear his overexuberance, his willingness to presume the nature of another's identity, a habit he practices in the present moment of the narrative as well in his lack of cross-racial understanding of Hickman. The failure of McIntyre's relationship with Laura, then, is a testament to the difficulty of the signal challenge Ellison sets before us in the second novel: the challenge of interracial empathy, of seeing the other in the self.[17]

McIntyre's relationship with Laura comes to an end when he finds himself unable to stand up for their love when it counts the most: in front of Laura's mother (and the impending threat presented by Laura's father). Flaunting his interracial love in front of whites is an act of daring, doing so in front of blacks—and in particular, the black parents of his lover—proves more than McIntyre can sustain. What is left when the relationship ends, McIntyre reveals, is the memory not of love but rather of self-empowerment and boldness.

> Actually, I could hardly remember the sensation of love, the thrill of being with Laura, or the sense of release and power-over-life which she had afforded me. I did realize that the sense of daring which I had felt had come not so much from the unabashed gratification of forbidden emotions, but from the fact that the atmosphere in which we moved had then seemed to condone and encourage broad freedom of expression. For there life had seemed generally more openly expressive. Thoughts were uttered, actions were taken—even violent actions, erotic actions—with a facility and openness that was un-

known to my own background. But now, even as
these thoughts come painfully to me in an agony of
laughter, I realized that I had seen and experienced
only part of the truth.[18]

The truth that remains for McIntyre to discover—the
truth of complex life behind the guise of stereotype—somehow rests in the mystery now before him. Presented in a period
of two days with the host of experiences across the color line,
from McMillen, Rockmore, and Duval to LeeWillie Minifees
and the burning Cadillac, to Sunraider and Hickman, he realizes that he has "touched another world."

The most fully rendered female character Ellison would ever
write is Janey Glover. Not coincidentally, the fullest, most authentic love story he would ever write concerns Janey and Ellison's protagonist from the second novel, Alonzo Hickman.
Ellison appears to have conceived Janey as an independent
figure, an equal to Hickman and to anyone else in the manuscripts. He asserts the force of her personality and the depth of
her feeling in a series of critical episodes that entwine themselves around the core narrative.

Janey first catches Hickman's attention when they are
both young, when Hickman is a roving jazz musician and she
a young woman in the bloom of her beauty. They fall out of
touch, only to be thrust back together through a web of circumstances involving Hickman's estranged surrogate child,
Bliss, who passes through the small town in Oklahoma in
which Janey lives long enough to begin filming a movie and se-
duce a young woman named Lavatrice. When Lavatrice discovers that she is pregnant by the stranger, she seeks out Janey.
After giving birth, Lavatrice takes her own life, and Janey is left

to raise the child, a boy she names Severen. In the years that
follow, Janey never marries, partly, we are to surmise, out of
her lovesick longing for Hickman and partly out of her single-
minded dedication to Severen and the other young boys she
takes in to raise. Janey's "little men" also include a boy named
Cliofus, a kind of savant who grows up to become a nightclub
storyteller and chronicler of experience. When Bliss, now Sunraider, intercedes to move his young son to boarding school,
the trauma causes a wound that never heals.

In the present moment of the narrative, Severen has returned, now a young man in his twenties, to the Oklahoma of
his youth. Although he makes no direct appearance in the narrative (though he does in fragmentary drafts not included in
Three Days Before the Shooting . . .), it seems that he returns to
get the full story of his birth, his mother's death, and, most of
all, his father. He seeks revenge on the man whom he believes
has stolen from him, not once but twice, the only women who
love him. The seed of the narrative action comes when Janey
sends a frantic letter to her long-estranged love, Hickman, in
which she alludes in broad but troubling terms to the "little
man" and the trouble he wishes to stir up. She fears for Bliss's
life at the hands of his estranged son, and she begs Hickman
for help. The irony is that Hickman's efforts to save Bliss, now
Sunraider, actually end up bringing about his murder by leading Severen to his target.

At its best, Ellison's second novel achieves a lucidity, a
force of eloquence unfamiliar even in the pages of *Invisible
Man*. His greatest improvisations on the computer, particularly those departures that take him away from familiar fictional ground, are among the most emotionally bare writings
Ellison produced. Within them he attends to themes left largely
unconsidered elsewhere in his fiction—even in earlier incar-

nations of the second novel. Notable among these is love, both
filial and romantic, a theme he explores through the rich voice
of Alonzo Hickman. In a scene from the computer, a file
named "Decision" from the Georgia & Oklahoma section of
Three Days Before the Shooting . . . , Ellison describes the moment when Hickman first lays eyes on Janey, the woman he
would come to love. It is a reverie written in the second person.
The passage is a remarkable discovery for those familiar only
with *Invisible Man* and *Juneteenth;* Ellison evinces particular
qualities of sensuality and vulnerability to go along with the
humor and stylistic command familiar from his past work.
Taking his jazz-inflected style to new heights, Ellison renders
Hickman's trombone solo as a playful exchange between two
voices, two impulses. From the marvelous turns of trombone
"sweet talk" now made manifest in language to the rhythmic
invention that surges and swells, contracts and expands, the
passage is a testament to Ellison's creative vision and stylistic
invention in the last years of his life. Here we are witness to an
author still in command of his craft, a master whose control is
matched by his daring virtuosity. This is Ellison writing past
his plan, past myth and symbol, past even *himself* in a way perhaps possible for him only in the lawless territory of fiction at
the dawn of the digital age. Strangely, it also hearkens backward, to the emergent spirit of his earliest efforts at fiction, the
impulse that inspired his greatest living achievement, *Invisible
Man.* The end was in the beginning.

VI

1945

In the spring of 1945, as World War II was drawing to a close and the world was just beginning to remake itself, Ralph Ellison began work on what would become, nearly seven years later, the only novel he would publish. In a letter addressed to Peggy Hitchcock of Reynal and Hitchcock, Ellison's publisher at the time, he defined the contours of the new literary philosophy taking shape in his imagination. He wished to write a "political allegory of everyday life" concerning a young Negro who moves from a small college in the rural South to the streets of New York. Though his novel contained much that would stretch credulity, Ellison insisted that it was not fantasy but intensified reality. As he would explain in his brief introduction to the excerpt of the novel published in 1948, his book was "to be read as a near-allegory or an extended metaphor. Indeed, its 'truth' lies precisely in its 'allegory' rather than in its 'facts.' The facts in themselves are of no moment, are, for me, even amusing. And for all the detailed description of the prose, the aim is not naturalism but realism—a realism dilated to deal with the almost surreal state of our everyday American life."[1]

Dilated realism would become the governing philosophy of Ellison's fiction, not simply for *Invisible Man* but for the second novel as well. Related but distinct from the philosophy of surrealism then in vogue, Ellison's dilated realism sought to harness the power of surrealism's transformative capacity while still rendering a recognizable everyday experience. In an interview just months after *Invisible Man*'s publication, he amplified his commitment to the principle. "I didn't select the surrealism, the distortion, the intensity, as an experimental technique, but because reality is surreal," he explained.[2]

In laying claim to realism, albeit a realism of a separate kind, Ellison distinguished his methods from pure surrealism. He had experimented with surrealism in early fiction, such as his short story "King of the Bingo Game." But what he aimed to do in *Invisible Man* would not fit so neatly into that category. Arnold Rampersad argues that the surrealism Ellison displayed in "King of the Bingo Game" would be "subtly modulated throughout *Invisible Man* and as crucial as any other aspect of form to its success." He goes on to assert that "a measure of surrealism suffuses all of *Invisible Man*. Absolutes, even those of time and place, are constantly in flux, agitated by the consciousness of the novel's naïve, increasingly neurotic, and to some extent unhinged if not deranged narrator." Although "surrealism" as a term offers a descriptive approximation for the atmosphere of some of *Invisible Man*'s most vivid passages, it fails to account fully for Ellison's fictive intent. Ellison finally rejects surrealism as thoroughly as he does social realism or naturalism. For him, the hybridized form of dilated realism was the only one suited to describe the reality he wished to portray.[3]

Inherent in the concept of dilated realism is an awareness of the limitations of realism alone to render in fiction a faithful picture of lived experience. Dilated realism does not sever reality entirely from its moorings; rather, it expands it in such a way that reality can encompass the fantastic while maintaining its plausible integrity. Rejecting naturalism's sometimes slavish adherence to mimetic representation, dilated realism would evoke experience as much as describe it. It would expand or contract its conception of the real not out of rote repetition but out of a desire to approach the experience of being. Just as the pupil of the human eye is still a pupil even when it expands and contracts with variations in light, so too is realism still realism even when it expands and contracts with variations in life.

In writing *Invisible Man* Ellison enlisted himself in an aesthetic movement with roots in the late nineteenth century and branches stretching through the revolutionary innovations of the modernists in the early twentieth century. Abstract Expressionist painters, like the Impressionists before them, responded to the limitation of realism when compared to photographers' lens by developing styles that reflected visual experience without relying on replication alone. In literature, James Joyce, Gertrude Stein, Virginia Woolf, William Faulkner, and many others employed narrative strategies that approached the experience of consciousness in language. And then there were the social realists, writers such as Richard Wright, who borrowed from the Dreiserian school in seeking to capture human life through close attention to physical experience. Ellison's dilated realism as it achieves itself in *Invisible Man* and as it refines itself in the second novel is something else altogether, an attempt to jar the reader into awareness and association by juxtaposing the familiar with the absurd.

In addition to writing in favor of a particular aesthetic perspective, Ellison was at least implicitly writing against another—Wright's social realism. As Lawrence Jackson notes, the composition of *Invisible Man* saw Ellison reject hard-boiled realism in favor of abstract symbolism. Although *Invisible Man* had struck many readers as avant-garde, Ellison would caution in his acceptance speech for the National Book Award that it was nonetheless a novel steeped in classical themes: the struggle for freedom and identity. *Invisible Man* simultaneously draws on the ur-traditions of the novel in Western literature— the picaresque, the *Küntslerroman*—even as it extended the boundaries of literary expression.[4]

The concept of dilated realism was undoubtedly forged in the crucible of its time, in the milieu of New York leftist intellectuals and activists with whom Ellison associated as well as among the ordinary black citizens whom he interviewed during his research for the Federal Writer's Project. It no doubt responds, in ways both replicative and reactionary, to literary naturalism. And it draws inspiration, as does the novel it would ultimately help animate, from a host of sources both literary and philosophical, European and American. This intellectual heritage, the history of Ellison's idea, offers a way into his compositional practice, both how it would evolve over decades and how it remained surprisingly consistent, despite radical shifts in the social and cultural contexts to which he was seeking to respond.[5]

It is no simple matter of semantics that Ellison displaces surrealism from the realm of artistic technique to the nature of experience itself. Dilated realism as Ellison would come to understand it was not a representational choice of the artist but a state of being in a world gone topsy-turvy. The very concept, then, is a kind of protest in that it refuses to relinquish its claims to reality even as it renders the absurd. Dilated realism was not simply an aesthetic technique or a philosophical posture but a practical tool for communication. It would prove one of the cornerstones of Ellison's imaginative perspective, a fitting paradigm not only for *Invisible Man* but for much of the fiction Ellison would compose during his lifetime, including, most provocatively, his long-labored second novel.

Ellison followed this principle of dilated realism throughout the second novel's protracted composition. Although the concept would adjust to fit contemporary circumstance, the basic features would remain. More than four decades after his letter to Peggy Hitchcock, Ellison reiterated his concept of dilated realism for his second novel, then already more than twenty years in progress. In a sprawling interview—really more of a collaborative essay—with James Alan McPherson entitled "Indivisible Man" and published in the December 1970 issue of the *Atlantic,* Ellison describes his novel as "realism extended beyond realism." Like *Invisible Man* and its dilated realism, the second novel's brand of realism would move between scenes of near-absurd extremes and those of a more prosaic cast. It would seek its representation of reality through the creative fusion of improvised forms.[6]

From his notes and correspondence as well as from the working drafts of *Invisible Man,* Ellison's dilated realism appears to have been a literary perspective born of necessity rather than of philosophy. His brand of surrealism was not a form of abstract protest or a matter of stylistic experimentation but a practical means of rendering the patent absurdity of racial discrimination both to those who experienced it themselves and to those who denied its potency. Fittingly, it would be a technique that built in its own obsolescence; the core dilated theme of invisibility loses power in a world of racial harmony. Ellison often said that he didn't imagine *Invisible Man* would last. "It's not an important novel," he told interviewers in "The Art of Fiction." "I failed of eloquence, and many of the immediate issues are rapidly fading away. If it does last, it will simply be because there are things going on in its depth that are of more permanent interest than on its surface. I hope so, anyway."[7]

As the circumstances of race relations in the United States improve, could it be that the utility of Ellison's technique of dilated realism and, with it, the social relevance of *Invisible Man* might diminish as well? Kenneth Warren approaches this claim in his reassessment of *Invisible Man*. He argues provocatively that if Ellison speaks for us today, it is because we are still mired in calcified patterns of racial thinking. "Taking seriously Ellison's democratic hopes," Warren writes, "may be to imagine a world in which *Invisible Man* no longer speaks immediately to us or for us as a way of investigating contemporary American identity." Ellison's writing is not simply proscriptive or documentary but paradigmatic. *Invisible Man* is relevant today not because we have failed to move beyond Jim Crow race logic but because Ellison saw beyond Jim Crow himself to a future of new possibilities.[8]

Critical to the proper function of Ellison's dilated realism in fiction are transitions between scenes because these provide the pivot points that enable the contraction and expansion of reality in his fiction. Ellison composed episodically, so transitions had great significance in his compositional process. Time and again throughout his notes as well as in many of his published remarks about the craft of fiction, he underscores the particular challenge transitions presented to him. In an address delivered at the Library of Congress in 1964, published in

Shadow and Act as "Hidden Name and Complex Fate," Ellison specifically addresses the relation between transitions and dilated realism. "I find that a sense of the ritual understructure of the fiction helps guide the creation of characters," he explains. "Action is the thing. We are what we do and do not do. The problem for me is to get from A to B to C. My anxiety about transitions greatly prolonged the writing of my book. The naturalists stick to case histories and sociology and are willing to compete with the camera and the tape recorder. I despise correctness in writing, but when reality is deranged in fiction, one must worry about the seams." Here Ellison is not only rejecting naturalism ("I despise correctness in writing") but describing the heightened responsibility a writer of his particular cast of mind must take for his fiction. When realism is dilated or, as he puts it here, when "reality is deranged in fiction," the writer must take great pains in composing the narrative chronology, given that this chronology is likely not simply a linear one. Naturalism, in other words, carries with it an external logic of order; dilated realism must forge that logic from within, out of the artist's specific vision of experience. The burden is on the writer to fit the various scraps of fiction together into a whole. Like a tailor sewing a garment, the writer must work the seams in such a way that they bind the pieces without calling attention to themselves.[9]

Transitions mattered to Ellison because they were the means by which he arranged action in his fiction, the fundamental challenge of communication in fiction as Ellison understood it. In other words, transitions were the primary means by which a writer collaborated with an audience in making meaning through fiction. In an undated handwritten note he articulates this bedrock literary philosophy in a passage worth quoting at length:

A writer's art consists of his ability to manipulate
the conventions of his craft, and he does so on various levels much as a juggler gives long hours of
practice to the task of keeping his India clubs flying
its to and fro from hand to air to hand and back to
hand according to a predetermined pattern. Of
course writing is more complex because the writer
seeks to convey ideas as well as images and actions.
And he tries to make his ideas emerge *through* his
arrangements of action and images, through tempo
and details of description and through presenta-
tions of psychology which bring his characters alive
in the mind of his readers. Here he values the in-
formed reader, the reader skilled in reading, because
he must communicate with mere words on a page;
and he achieves communication by encouraging
the reader to cooperate by using his, the reader's,
imagination and knowledge of other fiction and
forms of storytelling to bring the story alive. When
this happens, when the reader feels that he is "experiencing" the story, the writer is most successful in
communicating his vision of experience.

Ellison's ideas emerged through the aid of strong transitions,
the means by which he arranged actions and images, mastered
tempo, and communicated psychological truth. Ellison's greatest achievement in "communicating his vision of experience"
is, of course, *Invisible Man,* and *Invisible Man*'s most indelible
act of communication is its epilogue. The epilogue, a late in-
novation in the novel's compositional history, would prove the
novel's capstone. The clarity of its expression and soberness of
its tone would ironically reinforce the dilated realism more

commonly associated with the deranged reality of the battle royal, the paint factory, or, perhaps most powerfully, the wild riot that finally drives the novel's protagonist belowground and the castration nightmare that closes the final chapter. The epilogue presents a stark break in the novel's tone as well as in its narrative progression. Its purpose is at once one of resumption—bringing the reader back to the time present established in the prologue—and of transformation—marking a number of fundamental shifts in thought and feeling. With it, Ellison achieves his highest aspiration in fiction: to render a realism dilated to account for the surreal nature of American life.[10]

It is difficult to imagine *Invisible Man* without its epilogue, and yet by the summer of 1950, Ralph Ellison had an 868-page manuscript with no conclusion. Instead, the narrative ended abruptly with a wild riot in Harlem followed by Invisible Man's surreal nightmare of castration and the loss of "illusion." After awakening in the darkness of the underground he realizes the impossibility of returning to his aboveground life. "Here, at least," he asserts, "I could try to think things out in peace, or, if not in peace, in quiet. I would take up residence underground. The end was in the beginning."[11]

In the months that followed, Ellison revised the novel with the assistance of an informal editorial team, including his editor at Random House, Albert Erskine; his friend Harry Ford, an editor at Knopf; and his intellectual sparring partner and fellow Burkean, Stanley Edgar Hyman. As Ellison biographer Lawrence Jackson notes, "Ellison began to eliminate excess heft from the manuscript; significant tightening of the novel took place in 1950." Among the most important changes Ellison made was fashioning an epilogue. The epilogue, along

e Man recalls how it would become his sole source of
ort during moments of acute invisibility. His own grow-
ophistication in responding to Leroy's entries becomes
ometer of his political enlightenment. The journal pro-
Invisible Man with a theoretical handbook and self-
ovement manual. It takes its place among his treasured
s and, as late in composition as the novel's original type-
t, it is the only item salvaged when he resorts to burning
contents of his briefcase to light his way through the
rground.

Leroy's journal offered Ellison a means of shoring up the
l's ideological foundation. The published novel achieves
mainly through the epilogue, augmented by a few key re-
ive passages in the body of the narrative. One could make
case that this is a more organic means of rendering such
tent; certainly it is a less obtrusive one. By weighting the
ology to the epilogue, Ellison liberates the rest of the narra-
to flow unburdened by dogma. As an apprentice writer,
ticularly one schooled among Marxist authors and Richard
ight in particular, it would seem natural for Ellison to be
pted to tell more than show. But by extricating most of
telling to the extremes of the manuscript, Ellison liberates
showing. Although Leroy's journal is compelling reading,
th for its own content and for Invisible Man's running gloss
it, it would undoubtedly have had a leadening effect on the
rrative. Action grinds to a halt when an author employs such
ransparently ideological device. Ellison ultimately seems to
ve decided that the journal was too artificial, but he none-
eless salvages much of its content by giving the words, some-
mes verbatim, to Invisible Man. By rolling Leroy into Invisi-
e Man, Ellison internalizes Invisible Man's struggle between

with the prologue, would forcefully articulate the novel's core
intellectual principles while bounding its picaresque episodes
in a clear temporal frame. Its function, therefore, was both formal and thematic, completing the novel's structure while extending its central ideas.[12]

Only ten pages long, the epilogue somehow balances the
ideological weight of the entire novel on its slender frame. Invisible Man's belief in American pluralism becomes emblematic of the very process Ellison's readers have just experienced.
A young black man has just spoken to—and *for*—us in such a
way that we are implicated in his fate, just as citizens in a diverse nation are bound together in an inescapable network of
mutuality. We are, in other words, conditioned by the novel's
form and narrative voice to accept the epilogue's grand democratic claims.

A number of recent critics, however, seem inclined to
read the epilogue as artificial, as Ellison's self-conscious effort
to infuse the novel with sociopolitical significance. Some argue
that Ellison stacks the ideological deck, making claims for
American democratic faith that the rest of the novel does not
support. Others call attention to what they read as Ellison's
conflation of authorial and narratival voices. Still others, such
as Marxist critic Barbara Foley, go so far as to suggest that Ellison included the epilogue as ideological cover to protect himself from those who might question his political allegiance in
an atmosphere of red-baiting or as a means of cashing in on
the new spirit of aesthetic humanism then in vogue. Regardless of the relative merits of these critical interpretations, they
leave no doubt that the epilogue remains one of the novel's
most contested sections.[13]

As an improvised form, the epilogue lends itself to an exploration of its textual history. Tracing its origins in *Invisible*

Man's manuscripts leads to a number of discoveries that shed light on some of the elements of its style and modes of thought that have most confounded critics. To read the drafts is to witness a drama played out in which a young artist's evolving sense of aesthetic and ideological purpose is tested against the constraints of form and the expanse of his imagination. Ellison's habit of episodic composition combined with his high standards of craft meant that he worked at a deliberate pace. It also meant that, despite what he may have sketched out ahead of time in outlines or tables of contents, the narrative trajectory of his novel remained fluid until the very last moment. Were it not for his invention of the prologue and epilogue, as well as the several hundred pages he cut from the manuscript as it neared completion, one could imagine Ellison writing a boundless novel, with its protagonist in perpetual motion through a mounting series of incidents. It is not too much to say, then, that *Invisible Man* would never have achieved the status of an American classic were it not for those acts of excision that brought it into its present form.

Of course, it is obvious for any work of fiction that it takes its shape from what its author removes as well as from what he or she leaves in. The difference in this case is that much of what Ellison removed still doggedly asserts itself on the novel in ways that are perhaps indiscernible at first but no less indelible. *Invisible Man* is haunted by a host of invisible characters, characters he removed from the novel either because he feared their presence would distract the reader's focus from the narrator or because they seemed less a personality than an ideological crutch or even because they simply did not fit within the narrative flow. Ellison responded in various ways, sometimes removing characters entirely, at other times folding them into a composite, at still other times giving their

words or ideas to his protagonist. N
parent than in the textual history of th
acter of Leroy, who, though erased fr
asserts himself in some of *Invisible*
passages.

Reading the epilogue back thr
more than just a diverting critical exe
logue and, indeed, the entire novel, in
context while highlighting the evolutio
theme of democratic faith. Doing so de
tations of the novel as published but r
different questions of the material, to s
any other section of the novel, the epilo
its literary genesis. It owes much of its ri
Ellison's early drafts and, most especiall
ary conceit that he would later remove: L

Leroy's journal was one of Ellison'
for the manuscript. Less a character than
a former boarder at Mary Rambo's room
in the room Invisible Man comes to occup
cently drowned at sea, Leroy remains activ
a memory in the minds of Mary and her b
a personal journal he leaves behind in th
himself on Invisible Man's consciousness t
other characters, through his collection of
belongings (at Mary's urging, Invisible Ma
for a while), and, most powerfully, through

Invisible Man looks on Leroy's journa
by turns dumbfounded by Leroy's audacity
the echoes he hears of his own predicamen
in Invisible Man's slow process of self-recog
offers a profound stimulus. Looking back or

radical thought and status quo previously externalized in the conceit of the journal.

Sometime in the summer of 1950 Ellison sent a working draft of *Invisible Man* to his friend Harry Ford, an editor at Knopf. Among Ford's numerous suggestions was that Ellison eliminate Leroy's journal. "Careful reading leads me to feel quite strongly that Leroy's diary should be dropped entirely," he wrote in a two-page, single-spaced letter. "Prolix, didactic and inimical to the narrative—a crutch for the narrator which never entirely works (at least to this reader), and which remains simply a device. It seems to me that either Leroy has to be introduced as a *character* (if it is really necessary to project his highly sophisticated viewpoint) or eliminated entirely. I would prefer the latter." The implications of erasing Leroy were manifold. Ford continued by arguing that "if Leroy goes, then it seems to me that Mary has no reason for being, and all passages relevant should be deleted. I would see this as an invaluable tightening of the narrative, which is much too loose and shifty from here on." This critique is fascinating because of how Ellison would ultimately respond to the textual problem Ford identifies here. Leroy's journal comes across as a "device" rather than an organic expression of narrative, Ford argues. Ellison would ultimately agree, erasing Leroy from the manuscript. Yet Ellison would reject Ford's criticism of the substance of Leroy's message—that its "highly sophisticated viewpoint" would be better off excluded—and, in fact, he would bring certain elements of that viewpoint more integrally into the manuscript, with Invisible Man giving voice to some of Leroy's ideas. He would also keep Mary Rambo, though her role would be dramatically reduced. In doing so, he telescopes the intellectual content, leaving out many of the extended meditations on political issues.[14]

To read Leroy's journal is to read a fun-house version of Invisible Man's deepest pondering from the prologue and epilogue. It is to witness some of the novel's indelible passages incongruously reset in organic yet unfamiliar contexts. It is to participate in the excavation of ideas, at different times extending and undercutting the central assertions of the published novel.

Although Ellison's decision to exclude Leroy's journal was undoubtedly a stylistic one, it had considerable thematic implications. Without Leroy's journal, *Invisible Man* retains only one political philosophy that the novel accepts: the emerging democratic creed of the protagonist, stated most emphatically in the novel's final pages. Over the course of the narrative, Ellison introduces and rejects a series of competing political worldviews, from Bledsoe's killer accommodationism to Ras's self-destructive black nationalism to Rinehart's politics of chaos and invisibility and finally, most emphatically, to the Brotherhood's venal brand of Marxism. There is no room for any of these in the novel, and in fact, Invisible Man's rejection of each defines critical moments in his development as a character. In the end, they define the boundaries of his emergent humanism, the novel's sane alternative to the madness that abounds elsewhere.

But how did Ellison, who had honed his craft writing for leftist periodicals and kept company among avowed Communists, find himself writing a novel that makes so many claims for American diversity and principle? Lucas E. Morel, a political philosopher, insists that *Invisible Man* is a novel of politics, uniquely centered on American practice and principle. "At bottom," he writes, "*Invisible Man* is a book for citizens, espe-

lectual content, leaving out many of the extended meditations on political issues.[14]

To read Leroy's journal is to read a fun-house version of Invisible Man's deepest pondering from the prologue and epilogue. It is to witness some of the novel's indelible passages incongruously reset in organic yet unfamiliar contexts. It is to participate in the excavation of ideas, at different times extending and undercutting the central assertions of the published novel.

Although Ellison's decision to exclude Leroy's journal was undoubtedly a stylistic one, it had considerable thematic implications. Without Leroy's journal, *Invisible Man* retains only one political philosophy that the novel accepts: the emerging democratic creed of the protagonist, stated most emphatically in the novel's final pages. Over the course of the narrative, Ellison introduces and rejects a series of competing political worldviews, from Bledsoe's killer accommodationism to Ras's self-destructive black nationalism to Rinehart's politics of chaos and invisibility and finally, most emphatically, to the Brotherhood's venal brand of Marxism. There is no room for any of these in the novel, and in fact, Invisible Man's rejection of each defines critical moments in his development as a character. In the end, they define the boundaries of his emergent humanism, the novel's sane alternative to the madness that abounds elsewhere.

But how did Ellison, who had honed his craft writing for leftist periodicals and kept company among avowed Communists, find himself writing a novel that makes so many claims for American diversity and principle? Lucas E. Morel, a political philosopher, insists that *Invisible Man* is a novel of politics, uniquely centered on American practice and principle. "At bottom," he writes, "*Invisible Man* is a book for citizens, espe-

radical thought and status quo previously externalized in the conceit of the journal.

Sometime in the summer of 1950 Ellison sent a working draft of *Invisible Man* to his friend Harry Ford, an editor at Knopf. Among Ford's numerous suggestions was that Ellison eliminate Leroy's journal. "Careful reading leads me to feel quite strongly that Leroy's diary should be dropped entirely," he wrote in a two-page, single-spaced letter. "Prolix, didactic and inimical to the narrative—a crutch for the narrator which never entirely works (at least to this reader), and which remains simply a device. It seems to me that either Leroy has to be introduced as a *character* (if it is really necessary to project his highly sophisticated viewpoint) or eliminated entirely. I would prefer the latter." The implications of erasing Leroy were manifold. Ford continued by arguing that "if Leroy goes, then it seems to me that Mary has no reason for being, and all passages relevant should be deleted. I would see this as an invaluable tightening of the narrative, which is much too loose and shifty from here on." This critique is fascinating because of how Ellison would ultimately respond to the textual problem Ford identifies here. Leroy's journal comes across as a "device" rather than an organic expression of narrative, Ford argues. Ellison would ultimately agree, erasing Leroy from the manuscript. Yet Ellison would reject Ford's criticism of the substance of Leroy's message—that its "highly sophisticated viewpoint" would be better off excluded—and, in fact, he would bring certain elements of that viewpoint more integrally into the manuscript, with Invisible Man giving voice to some of Leroy's ideas. He would also keep Mary Rambo, though her role would be dramatically reduced. In doing so, he telescopes the intel-

visible Man recalls how it would become his sole source of comfort during moments of acute invisibility. His own growing sophistication in responding to Leroy's entries becomes a barometer of his political enlightenment. The journal provides Invisible Man with a theoretical handbook and self-improvement manual. It takes its place among his treasured items and, as late in composition as the novel's original typescript, it is the only item salvaged when he resorts to burning the contents of his briefcase to light his way through the underground.

Leroy's journal offered Ellison a means of shoring up the novel's ideological foundation. The published novel achieves this mainly through the epilogue, augmented by a few key reflective passages in the body of the narrative. One could make the case that this is a more organic means of rendering such content; certainly it is a less obtrusive one. By weighting the ideology to the epilogue, Ellison liberates the rest of the narrative to flow unburdened by dogma. As an apprentice writer, particularly one schooled among Marxist authors and Richard Wright in particular, it would seem natural for Ellison to be tempted to tell more than show. But by extricating most of the telling to the extremes of the manuscript, Ellison liberates the showing. Although Leroy's journal is compelling reading, both for its own content and for Invisible Man's running gloss on it, it would undoubtedly have had a leadening effect on the narrative. Action grinds to a halt when an author employs such a transparently ideological device. Ellison ultimately seems to have decided that the journal was too artificial, but he nonetheless salvages much of its content by giving the words, sometimes verbatim, to Invisible Man. By rolling Leroy into Invisible Man, Ellison internalizes Invisible Man's struggle between

words or ideas to his protagonist. Nowhere is this more apparent than in the textual history of the epilogue and the character of Leroy, who, though erased from the published novel, asserts himself in some of *Invisible Man*'s most important passages.

Reading the epilogue back through the typescripts is more than just a diverting critical exercise. It places the epilogue and, indeed, the entire novel, in its ancestral intellectual context while highlighting the evolution of Ellison's dominant theme of democratic faith. Doing so does not efface interpretations of the novel as published but rather directs us to ask different questions of the material, to see it anew. More than any other section of the novel, the epilogue bears the mark of its literary genesis. It owes much of its richness to its origins in Ellison's early drafts and, most especially, to a particular literary conceit that he would later remove: Leroy's journal.

Leroy's journal was one of Ellison's last significant cuts for the manuscript. Less a character than a conceit, Leroy was a former boarder at Mary Rambo's rooming house who lived in the room Invisible Man comes to occupy. Though he has recently drowned at sea, Leroy remains active in the narrative as a memory in the minds of Mary and her boarders and through a personal journal he leaves behind in the house. He asserts himself on Invisible Man's consciousness through the words of other characters, through his collection of books and personal belongings (at Mary's urging, Invisible Man wears his clothes for a while), and, most powerfully, through the journal.

Invisible Man looks on Leroy's journal in amazed regard, by turns dumbfounded by Leroy's audacity and transfixed by the echoes he hears of his own predicament. As a plot device in Invisible Man's slow process of self-recognition, the journal offers a profound stimulus. Looking back on its discovery, In-

Man's manuscripts leads to a number of discoveries that shed light on some of the elements of its style and modes of thought that have most confounded critics. To read the drafts is to witness a drama played out in which a young artist's evolving sense of aesthetic and ideological purpose is tested against the constraints of form and the expanse of his imagination. Ellison's habit of episodic composition combined with his high standards of craft meant that he worked at a deliberate pace. It also meant that, despite what he may have sketched out ahead of time in outlines or tables of contents, the narrative trajectory of his novel remained fluid until the very last moment. Were it not for his invention of the prologue and epilogue, as well as the several hundred pages he cut from the manuscript as it neared completion, one could imagine Ellison writing a boundless novel, with its protagonist in perpetual motion through a mounting series of incidents. It is not too much to say, then, that *Invisible Man* would never have achieved the status of an American classic were it not for those acts of excision that brought it into its present form.

Of course, it is obvious for any work of fiction that it takes its shape from what its author removes as well as from what he or she leaves in. The difference in this case is that much of what Ellison removed still doggedly asserts itself on the novel in ways that are perhaps indiscernible at first but no less indelible. *Invisible Man* is haunted by a host of invisible characters, characters he removed from the novel either because he feared their presence would distract the reader's focus from the narrator or because they seemed less a personality than an ideological crutch or even because they simply did not fit within the narrative flow. Ellison responded in various ways, sometimes removing characters entirely, at other times folding them into a composite, at still other times giving their

with the prologue, would forcefully articulate the novel's core intellectual principles while bounding its picaresque episodes in a clear temporal frame. Its function, therefore, was both formal and thematic, completing the novel's structure while extending its central ideas.[12]

Only ten pages long, the epilogue somehow balances the ideological weight of the entire novel on its slender frame. Invisible Man's belief in American pluralism becomes emblematic of the very process Ellison's readers have just experienced. A young black man has just spoken to—and *for*—us in such a way that we are implicated in his fate, just as citizens in a diverse nation are bound together in an inescapable network of mutuality. We are, in other words, conditioned by the novel's form and narrative voice to accept the epilogue's grand democratic claims.

A number of recent critics, however, seem inclined to read the epilogue as artificial, as Ellison's self-conscious effort to infuse the novel with sociopolitical significance. Some argue that Ellison stacks the ideological deck, making claims for American democratic faith that the rest of the novel does not support. Others call attention to what they read as Ellison's conflation of authorial and narratival voices. Still others, such as Marxist critic Barbara Foley, go so far as to suggest that Ellison included the epilogue as ideological cover to protect himself from those who might question his political allegiance in an atmosphere of red-baiting or as a means of cashing in on the new spirit of aesthetic humanism then in vogue. Regardless of the relative merits of these critical interpretations, they leave no doubt that the epilogue remains one of the novel's most contested sections.[13]

As an improvised form, the epilogue lends itself to an exploration of its textual history. Tracing its origins in *Invisible*

cially American citizens." In many ways, Morel and other critics are extending an interpretation of the novel first offered by Ellison himself. Just a year after the novel's publication, on receipt of the National Book Award, Ellison explained that *Invisible Man* had been an "attempt to return to the mood of personal moral responsibility for democracy which typified the best of our nineteenth-century fiction." He called for the American novel to "anticipate the resolution of those world problems of humanity which for the moment seem to those who are in awe of statistics completely insoluble." [15]

Decades later, Ellison would develop these same beliefs in the introduction to *Invisible Man*'s thirtieth-anniversary edition. Ellison portrays his novel as part of a grand tradition of American fiction with its roots in a nineteenth century supremely concerned with American identity and democracy. "So if the ideal of achieving a true political equality eludes us in reality—as it continues to do—there is still available that fictional *vision* of an ideal democracy in which the actual combines with the ideal and gives us representations of a state of things in which the highly placed and the lowly, the black and the white, the northerner and the southerner, the native born and the immigrant are combined to tell us of transcendent truths and possibilities." *Invisible Man,* therefore, is conceived as a "raft of hope, perception and entertainment that might help keep us afloat as we tried to negotiate the snags and whirlpools that mark our nation's vacillating course toward and away from the democratic ideal." This offers a powerful way of interpreting the novel; its appeal is so strong that it has the effect of blinding us to the reality of what Ellison actually wrote more than thirty years before this. Ellison is, in effect, teaching us how to read his novel and how not to read it as well.[16]

Invisible Man is a far more complex and equivocal expression of American ideals than Ellison's retrospective analysis would allow. A rift exists between the politics of the later Ellison and those of the Ellison of *Invisible Man*. What is most compelling is the degree to which his later politics, expressed in his numerous essays and public addresses, have affected critical interpretations of *Invisible Man*. Writing against this grain, Raymond A. Mazurek argues that traces of Ellison's youthful preoccupation with "working class politics" find their way into "his hopes for a pluralistic America that can overcome racism under the sign of democracy." The point of confluence, he argues, is *Invisible Man*. "It is his skepticism toward the left and his greater optimism for America that is new," Mazurek continues. "In *Invisible Man,* where the skepticism and optimism emerge, there remains an elegiac celebration of the political opposition movements of the popular front alongside Ellison's satirical portrayal of American Communism."[17]

Reading *Invisible Man* as a transitional political moment in Ellison's life marks the ideological midpoint between binaries: communism and democracy, opposition and establishment. In light of these seismic shifts in Ellison's personal politics and aesthetic vision, Leroy's journal has even greater implications for our understanding of the novel and Ellison's evolving political views. These changes did not occur in isolation; Ellison was undoubtedly affected by the Cold War political climate of the late 1940s and early 1950s. Writing of the crucial final stage of *Invisible Man*'s composition, Arnold Rampersad notes that "no factor kept him stumbling in the home stretch more than the political maelstrom then sweeping across American and the fact that he had once been a Communist sympathizer or an actual Communist. Viewed in the pages of newspapers and magazines, on radio and television, the Cold War pitted the Soviet Union and the international left against the United States and its anti-Communist nationalism." Such bright lines of division, however, did not govern Ellison's personal philosophies. Even so, he faced a number of challenging questions as he prepared the final draft of his manuscript. Rampersad offers the following: "How should these factors affect the composition of his novel? How might they affect its reception? What did he actually now believe about the right, the left, America, the Negro, and politics in general?"[18]

Leroy's journal, both its substance and its textual history inside and outside of the published novel, helps answer these questions. It provides a new way of understanding Ellison's Americanist faith, a faith that finds novelistic expression in the grand, incomplete design of his second novel, emerging from the more radical political ideology of Ellison's pre–*Invisible Man* days. Closely reading these expurgated portions of the manuscript reinforces Mazurek's contention that *Invisible Man* embodies the meeting of seemingly irreconcilable beliefs and their unity in the imaginative space of Ellison's fiction. The entire novel is a kind of ideological laboratory with Leroy as its most profound experiment.

Leroy's journal is in many ways a familiar modernist conceit, the found object constituting a text within a text. On a functional level it provides Ellison with the means to inject a tremendous amount of ideological content into a constricted narrative space. The cost, of course, is that it taxes the reader's suspension of disbelief and, consequently, threatens to disrupt narrative momentum. Ellison would finally decide that these costs were too great. In addition to those passages that Ellison would conserve and repurpose through Invisible Man's own

voice in the epilogue, several compelling sections from the
journal would never find their way into the published novel.
Their absence nonetheless shapes the novel, often as powerfully as their presence might have done.

Leroy's journal is a subversive text written into *Invisible
Man,* a kind of anarchical gloss on the ideology Ellison develops in the dominant narrative. The published novel itself is
clear in its ideological choices. It rejects Ras's black nationalism and, ultimately, the Brotherhood's political philosophy as
well. It asserts in the epilogue an ambivalent but palpable faith
in American democratic principle and the promise of a pluralistic future. Resisting determinism, it makes a strong case
for openness—even love—as the basis of politics.

On encountering the journal, Invisible Man quickly dis-
cerns that it is something of value. Flipping through its contents, he "began to encounter notes the like[s] of which I had
never seen or dreamed." The first offers Leroy's bold revision-
ist assessment of Frederick Douglass, taking him to task for
relying on words instead of deeds. After reading this first note,
Invisible Man is transfixed. "I could not believe my eyes,"
he writes. "This Leroy wrote like a criminal! Why he would
have been arrested for writing such crazy stuff. It sounded as
wild as the speech I had heard the West Indian shouting from
the step-ladder my first night in Harlem." Such a comparison
to Ras is calculated, meant less to reflect a substantive relation
between Leroy's incendiary ideas and Ras's discredited black
nationalist ravings, and more to comment on Invisible Man's
as-yet-unrefined powers of critical discernment. His initial response to the journals is naive, just as his trust in Bledsoe's
letter had been, or his youthful faith in the power of "right" be-
havior. This first section of Leroy's journal, one of two portions of text dedicated to it, thus takes on the function of a
compacted political training—much as Hambro's four-month

Brotherhood instruction of Invisible Man (which takes place outside of the narrative frame) will later serve in the published novel. The difference here is that Ellison has chosen to display the instruction, relying on the conceit that these disconnected excerpts can somehow stand in narrative time for a process of political awakening that undoubtedly would take much longer to achieve in real time. The text becomes Leroy's journal rather than Invisible Man's memoir, and the memoir enacts Invisible Man's consciousness as a critical reader of this other document.[19]

One of the most illuminating themes to emerge from Leroy's journal, though it makes no appearance in the published novel, is the concept of cosmopolitanism. *Invisible Man* is studied in its focus on the American context. With the exception of Ras's pan-Africanism, which the novel roundly caricatures, no examples of an international perspective survive in the novel. Leroy, however, emerges as a strong advocate of a global worldview that connects his own personal identity to a human network that extends well beyond national borders. Following the Frederick Douglass note, Invisible Man encounters the following, read "at random." "It is part of the character imposed upon us as a people," Invisible Man reads, "to be a 'race'—that vague term without cultural or geographical, or psychological boundaries—but it is my nature, my internal compulsion, to be a man, a member of a culture, a civilization, a citizen of the world. I am morally stronger than the most vicious mob because I believe in this idea." Rejecting race as the sole marker of identity, Leroy argues for a rebirth of individual identity that comes about, ironically, by asserting an even broader identity than race: the "citizen of the world." The passage implicitly criticizes race, not for being too broad to contain the individual as is often argued, but rather for being at once too "vague" and yet somehow too specific as well in an American context that recognizes blacks by little more than the color of their skin. Leroy posits an alternative conception of identity that, in effect, builds itself up from the most generic (albeit gender-biased) identity of "man" up through "culture," "civilization" (a political identity), to "citizen of the world," an identity that defines itself through both the autonomy of the liberated individual to move across all boundaries and the entrenchment of that individual in a collective identity that links him with his fellow human beings, regardless of distinctions. This is a more explicit statement of the "frightening" question that Invisible Man voices at the end of the published novel.[20]

The epilogue would be one of the last substantive additions Ellison made to the manuscript, and its shape would constitute a heteroglossic and improvised novelistic form. In its final iteration, it draws from numerous textual sources, including the prologue and, most ingeniously, Leroy's journal. By repurposing these passages, Ellison fashions an improvised but effective end to his novel. Even as the epilogue concludes the novel, it also develops an ideological agenda of its own. Though not wholly new to the manuscript, several of the epilogue's key concepts are nonetheless articulated with the greatest force and linked for the first time in these final pages.

Leroy's journal first appears in the typescripts just as Invisible Man is getting himself settled at Mary's, after his trouble at the paint factory and his surreal ordeal in the factory hospital's unidentified machine. He finds the book among the rows of recondite volumes near Leroy's bed. Over the next eight pages the draft includes eight excerpts of varying length from the journal. Periodically throughout the remainder of the manuscript Invisible Man consults the journal to provide him direction in his path to enlightenment. In all, Leroy's journal takes up three significant fragments of manuscript, around chapters 12, 14, and 16 in the published novel. As published, the first portion of text originally written for Leroy's journal comes on the eighth page of the epilogue. Two passages follow, the first as it appears in the published novel and the second as it appears in an undated draft of Leroy's journal.

> Since then [confronting Mr. Norton in the New York subway] I've sometimes been overcome with a passion to return to that "heart of darkness" across the Mason-Dixon line, but then I remind myself that the true darkness lies within my own mind, and the idea loses itself in the gloom. Still the passion persists. Sometimes I feel the need to reaffirm all of it, the whole unhappy territory and all the things loved and unlovable in it, for all of it is part of me. Till now, however, this is as far as I've ever gotten, for all life seen from the hole of invisibility is absurd.

> Sometimes, he wrote, I am overcome with the passion to return into the "heart of darkness" across the Mason Dixon Line, but then I always think that the true darkness lies within my own mind and the idea loses itself in the gloom.
>
> But still the passion persists. I feel the need to reaffirm all of it, the whole unhappy territory and all the things loved and unlovable, for all of it is part of me. ... Of course all of this is absurd, but then, all life is absurd. Perhaps when we recognize this we'll give up the attempt to escape from the familiar absurdity to one which we know naught of. A depressing thought this, for where then will progress lie?

These passages match up almost identically, with the only substantive addition being the final sentence of the passage from
the published novel contextualizing it within Invisible Man's
underground circumstance. The passage from Leroy's journal
is a complete entry taken from a long section in which Invisible Man reads randomly through the journal. It has no more
context than is seen here. It gives a strong sense of Leroy's
voice, the earnest profundity with which he paraphrases Ham-
let's famous soliloquy, something that would not be out of
place in Invisible Man's loquacious ramblings from the prologue. What we can see in this instance is how Invisible Man's
voice came to reflect certain elements of Leroy's voice. Speaking another character's words, even in a new context, cannot
help but shape the character's voice. If Invisible Man sounds
slightly different in the epilogue than he does in the rest of the
novel, it has a great deal to do with Leroy.[21]

Another example of how Ellison would recast Leroy's
words comes immediately after the passage from the published novel just quoted. This example, however, has a far more
entrenched place in its original context. Reading the passage in
Leroy's journal, it is hard to imagine it elsewhere. Again, consider the two passages together—the first from Leroy's journal,
the second from *Invisible Man*. The repurposed portion of
manuscript as it reads in the published novel begins with the
third sentence ("Without the possibility of action . . .").

> Without the possibility of action, all knowledge
> comes to one labeled 'file and forget'. I can neither
> file *or* forget. Nor will certain ideas forget me, they
> keep filing away at my lethargy, my complacency.
> Why should I be the one to dream this nightmare?

> So why do I write, torturing myself to put it down? Because in spite of myself I've learned some things. Without the possibility of action, all knowledge comes to one labeled 'file and forget,' and I can neither file nor forget. Nor will certain ideas forget me; they keep filing away at my lethargy, my complacency. Why should I be the one to dream this nightmare? Why should I be dedicated and set aside— yes, if not to at least *tell* a few people about it?

Ellison has reproduced the passage from Leroy's journal with little alteration. Building around it on both sides, he contextualizes it within Invisible Man's monologue. The passage now answers the question he asks himself in the opening line; it offers, in other words a rationale for writing. In the process of communication he finds utility and meaning for his experience, a reason for having undergone the nightmare of his life. This is the key insight of the epilogue, one that relies on the power of rhetoric, the power of voice to communicate on a mass scale.[22]

In their original context these words meant something else entirely. In Leroy's journal this paragraph concludes a lengthy story about Leroy's time as a butler for the mistress of a famous ambassador, a woman he simply calls Gabby. While in the woman's service, he observes a great deal—particularly related to the ambassador's personal and professional secrets and shames, including a glance into the man's diary, which offers "my first glimpse of diplomatic double-talk translated into plain English." He is free to witness all of this because he is so thoroughly underestimated by the whites who employ him. This leads him to a profound feeling of cynicism as to the function of political power. "It is a fallacy to say that people participate in their government," he concludes. "The people are *governed;* only those like Gabby participate—perhaps; the rest of us seldom get a glimpse." He then muses that "an essay on the private life of a diplomat written by his butler or his wife's maid would make history—and how!" Armed with his secret knowledge of the ambassador, Leroy is nonetheless rendered "without the possibility of action." Who would believe him? The passage refers to the futility of personal volition, not the necessity of collective voice as it is in the published version.

Unlike Invisible Man, Leroy does not resolve to take the next step; quite the contrary, he rejects the only step he mentions, the speculative dream of writing an essay on the private life of a diplomat. The tone of the passage, therefore, is one of defeat or at least temporary resignation. His final question resonates with horror. Ellison does not even allow Invisible Man to respond after reading the excerpt, instead having him explain that "before [he] could react to all this" he had come upon another note. Like so many of the entries in Leroy's journal, this one enacts a powerful drama in miniature that Elli-son finally leaves underutilized. By repurposing a portion of it as he has done in the epilogue he salvages the passage, though he does not carry over its specific dramatic context. Instead, he turns the passage in a markedly different, even oppositional, direction—toward tempered hope instead of outright resignation.

Most passages from Leroy's journal, however, did not find their way into the published manuscript. They tell an unexpected story, providing an alternative intellectual history and projecting a parallel but distinct fictive reality. What kind of novel would *Invisible Man* have been had Ellison chosen different passages from Leroy's journal for inclusion in the epilogue? How would the book change had Leroy's journal remained intact? These questions, of course, are conjectural, yet they may serve a practical purpose for criticism. They promise to excavate the ideological foundations of Ellison's novel during an extended period of its construction.

Reading Leroy back into *Invisible Man* requires recentering another character, Mary Rambo. Ellison's publication in 1963 of the extended transitional scene between the paint factory hospital and Mary's boardinghouse, "Out of the Hospital and Under the Bar," already suggests that Mary originally had a much larger role in the novel. "Old mary must embody a myth," Ellison scribbled in one of the hundreds of undated notes he wrote during the novel's protracted composition. Elsewhere he wrote that "she is the guardian of value." Like so many of the novel's secondary figures, Mary slips between character and archetype, existing on the picaresque narrative realm but finally embodying a symbol. Mary's role in the published novel has been reduced to the thinnest possible extent. She is present to reflect her dreams that Invisible Man will become a great leader, as well as to present him with the reality of what Ellison would elsewhere term the "pre-individualistic" state of the black masses. When Leroy was lost, so was much of Mary, if only because so many of the pages Ellison cut were set at Mary's boardinghouse. This meant that Ellison also cut the character of Cleo, Mary's niece and Leroy's lover, who becomes Invisible Man's love interest as well.[23]

Perhaps the greatest casualty that came of the excised sections at Mary's, however, is not a character but a theme: the novel's attention to political action. In a revealing note, Ellison describes the atmosphere at Mary's boardinghouse. "At Mary's they talk about making money, about music, about the 'race' and now increasingly they were concerned with politics and hard times. Long discussions were held in which it was debated whether there was real freedom in the north and what was the worst drawback to living in either region. There was also a great deal of talk about the evictions that were now taking place daily about Harlem. Groups were organizing and replacing furniture in evicted apartments." Of course, Ellison includes the scene of the eviction in which Invisible Man emerges as an orator, but the incident feels isolated rather than part of a social atmosphere that might be associated with any historical period. In cutting so many of the scenes at Mary Rambo's rooming house, and in losing the sense of improvised community created there, the novel sacrifices some of its political sensibility. Of course, in the process Ellison focuses his narrative more squarely on the internal experience of his nameless protagonist, and thus on the "universal" elements of human character. But in removing some of the texture of the political moment (the evictions, the types of conversations, and so on), the novel chooses a politics of ideology over practice, a politics of the individual over the group.[24]

The same certainly cannot be said of Leroy. Indeed, what makes Leroy's journal so incendiary is that it does so many things that *Invisible Man*'s critics have assumed Ellison was uninterested in or incapable of doing. It demonstrates a bold cosmopolitanist vision alive to the interconnectedness of global affairs rather than one more narrowly concentrated on the domestic. It speaks in radical, even revolutionary, terms that the published novel rejects, particularly in its handling of Ras the Exhorter. It offers a more nuanced and sophisticated alternative to Ras's parody of black nationalism. And finally, most profoundly for a novel Ellison would later characterize as a democratic "raft of hope," it looks with a far more critical and even pessimistic eye on the promise of American democracy.

Leroy served more than an expressly ideological purpose for Ellison's evolving manuscript. As Ellison conceived him, he would act as a kind of double for Invisible Man—helping to define his nameless protagonist by providing a baseline against which to measure Invisible Man's growing self-awareness. "You and Leroy are just alike," Cleo says to Invisible Man in one of their early encounters after his arrival at Mary's boardinghouse. Ellison builds this comparison not simply to develop Invisible Man's emerging relationship with Cleo but also to prepare the reader for the process of enlightenment and challenge that Leroy's journal is about to enact in Invisible Man's consciousness. Not long after this scene with Cleo Invisible Man finds himself alone in Leroy's old room, inspecting his bookshelf. He notices titles by Darwin, Freud, and Lord Raglan. "It might have been a room at college," he reflects, "only it was neater and the books more advanced, and seemed to have been thoroughly read, while at college they would have remained on the shelf unopened." This inspires a sense of inadequacy in Invisible Man. He explains, "I felt a twinge of resentment that this Leroy had read more than I." But just as he finally does after facing other challenges and seeming defeats, he responds, if belatedly, with action. In another draft Invisible Man explains his determination to "learn the meaning of the journal" and "read every book on the shelves" so that he would "know more than Leroy ever knew." The passage continues, with the bracketed portions representing an alternate rendering of the same passage from another of Ellison's numerous drafts of the scene. "And yet with this sense of rivalry I felt a dependence upon Leroy, for although he was drowned, he was the only influence I had ever encountered who justified the feelings that I had kept repressed within myself [my sense of invisibility]. I feared the effect of his journal, but during those days to follow when I was falling apart it was his attitude that kept me going [during those days to follow as I fell more thoroughly apart it was the journal that gave me a sense of reality]." The journal becomes a talisman for Invisible Man, its physical presence commanding his respect. Only Leroy's journal escapes incineration as Invisible Man lights his way through the underground using the contents of his briefcase. Beyond the journal's obvious interest to Invisible Man as the record of another's life, it embodies a rhetorical power that speaks to the particulars of his own invisibility.[25]

Yet for all of this, Ellison offers scant details of Leroy's identity in the manuscript drafts. We know that he was a boarder at Mary's, a merchant seaman who has recently drowned. We know that he was a favorite of all who lived at the house, and especially of Cleo, with whom he had a romantic relationship. We know, as evidenced by his journal entries, that he was a thinker of some depth and range, likely an autodidact, whose intellectual forays often took him to the limits of acceptability in public political discourse. In the most extended description of Leroy's character, Ellison offers the following notes:

> LeRoy is a young student who came North to study. An orphan he is self educated and distinctly different from those who like him were born in the South. He has learned to read, and has linked up his humanity with that of Humanity generally. He is interested in problems of leadership. He is Leader, psychologically, who had seen the dichotomy of his

position as consisting of a need to act on folk level, or of building up organization whereby he can operate on more sophisticated urban level. In folk he can see only limited possibilities, which are nevertheless vital. On the other hand he feels need to possess the meaning of the entire American culture, if not emotionally, intellectually—although he does not believe that such a division is necessary.

He is eligible for sacrifice because he could not satisfy Cleo (the sexual offense), because he is too ideal (the offense of the absolute), and because he fails in the interest of intellect to take some crucially necessary action.

In several crucial ways it could be a description of Invisible Man himself, with its emphasis on leadership, the goal of linking up "his humanity with that of Humanity generally," and the desire to "possess the meaning of the entire American culture." The difference, of course, is that, except for his desire to become a leader, Invisible Man comes to the rest of these late in the novel, really not until the epilogue. Ellison subjects Invisible Man to some of the same pitfalls as Leroy, seemingly making him "eligible for sacrifice" but ultimately giving him the strength to save himself. In the climactic dream that ends chapter 25, Invisible Man faces the loss of his illusions, and although he never approaches the "ideal," he nonetheless braces against it, and like Leroy, he grapples with the need to "take some crucially necessary action," which he finally resolves to do by preparing himself for the "next step" back aboveground.[26]

The novel's notes further suggest that Ellison was quite aware of the need to give Leroy a palpable presence in the novel. Throughout he admonishes himself to achieve this by relying on other characters' descriptions of him. "Leroy must do something for everyone at Mary's," he writes in an undated note. "For Mary he might be kind of son. For Cleo a lover, for Sam a younger version of himself. For Mrs. Garfield a shrewd man who has helped her collect insurance, etc." He would achieve most of this in a single long scene, a party all the key characters at Mary's house attend.

Ellison had decided to develop a friendship between Leroy and one roomer in particular, a man named Treadwell. It is to him that the following note likely refers.

> Roomer must have more complicated relationship with LeRoy. It must involve rejection-acceptance polarities. LeRoy is several things: Hero and scapegoat / Drowned sailor. / Promise of racial success and leadership. / The good man cut off in youth, in springtime of life. / The reaction of average semifolk Negro to such a type is mixed. For he feels all these things on the more or less subintellectual level, and while he cannot but hope for the success of this type, his experience has also taught him that they are prone to betrayal, snobbishness, irresponsibility. Only after LeRoy is drowned can her [sic] resolve his feelings and now he actually suffers.

When Ellison erased Leroy from the novel, he erased Invisible Man's potential double. Without the journal, Invisible Man has to come to an understanding of his invisibility on his own or, at the very least, by other means. Because of Leroy's absence, Invisible Man's relation to another young black man, the Brotherhood's Tod Clifton, would become even more pivotal. The contrast between the two is immediate and indelible. Ellison explains the relationship he wanted to establish in his notes, delineating Clifton's function as Invisible Man's double. "Contrasts with Clifton in order to bring out what? / He is markedly ambivilent [sic] while clifton [sic] is not/ He is reckless while Clifton is cautious / He is maniac [sic] while clifton [sic] is depressive/ He accepts brotherhood on face value while clifton [sic] questions motives of whites. / He accepts them wholeheartedly while clifton [sic] show them marked reserve. / Clifton physically handsome popular with members and community."[27]

In this series of oppositions Ellison underscores the answer to the rhetorical question he asks himself at the beginning of the note. The contrast with Clifton establishes the reasons why neither one could continue to exist in their present state. Clifton's fate is ultimately caught up in a dramatic, if indirect, act of personal destruction. Invisible Man seizes control of his own fate in part by witnessing Clifton's downfall. Clifton's devolution becomes a means for Invisible Man's transfiguration and a vehicle for the novel's resolution in the epilogue. In this way, Clifton's fate comes closest to serving the function Leroy's journal had served in previous drafts.

Elsewhere in Leroy's journal the germ of political ideology gets picked up again and taken in a startlingly new direction. In an extended excerpt, by far the longest Ellison would write from Leroy's journal, Leroy espouses a political philosophy of black domination that echoes Invisible Man's assertion in the epilogue that blacks are "responsible" for the fate of the nation because they are "somehow older" than white Americans. Radically extending Invisible Man's more measured claims, Leroy begins the entry with the assertion that "if there were a world of justice we would inherit the state through sheer default. Not because the humble ever inherit anything, but because we are alienated and forced into a position which makes us less susceptible to corruption." He enumerates the nature of black disenfranchisement. "Yet on the other hand," he continues, "we are forced into an identity of experience with the whole non-European world, with all those whose suffering is identified with their color." Later in the passage he picks up this same thread in audacious language.

> Could it be that we are the true inheritors of the West, the rightful heirs of its humanist tradition— especially since it has flourished through our own dehumanization, debasement, through our being ruled out of bounds; since we have been brutalized and forced to live inhuman lives so that they could become what they consider "more human"? Doesn't the pattern of our experience insist that we seek a way of life more universal, more human and more free than any to be found in the world today? . . . We must learn to accept and transform and depend upon the best there is in this West into which we have been born; we must learn to reject that which is false and only a continuation of our degradation.

This is an explicit assertion of a Pan-African or Third World politics that is unprecedented in Ellison's fiction and hardly more apparent in his nonfiction. Indeed, particularly in his later life, Ellison was outwardly hostile to suggestions that blacks had any greater connection to people of color around the world than to their fellow American citizens. Of course, it is faulty to compare the words of one character—especially one Ellison would ultimately erase—with the political convictions of the author, but it nonetheless speaks to a range of political thought that those familiar with Ellison's published corpus might be surprised to discover. Leroy is a character we are meant to respect because Invisible Man and everyone who has known him do. Leroy is ennobled by the manuscript, his ideas given credibility and force by dint of their eloquence and their emphasis.[28]

These powerful passages are nowhere to be found in *Invisible Man,* and yet something of their political substance remains in Invisible Man's extended consideration of "the principle" in the epilogue. In a lengthy passage, Ellison has Invisible Man voice a call to black conscience, a call to account not simply for the fate of black people in America but for the fate of the nation as a whole. Invisible Man grapples with the fundamental tensions among the powerful, the oppressed, and the principle of the nation's founding. Tied up in his grandfather's deathbed advice to "agree 'em to death and destruction" is what Ellison terms in his notes a "heritage of responsibility" that Invisible Man at first rejects, then reconsiders in the epilogue. [29]

But to what, Invisible Man is finally able to ask, is one to agree? He cycles through an array of responses. One could affirm the principle but not the people. One could affirm both principle and flawed people as the only means to transcendence—to turn the other cheek and love one's neighbor safe in the knowledge that suffering is redemptive. Would we do this because the experience of slavery and racial discrimination had tempered us, made us somewhat less susceptible to the pettiness that afflicts others? This is a dangerous possibility, because it suggests that racism might somehow be a boon to black people. Or should blacks affirm the principle simply because we are all Americans, and as a result are bound together in our fates with the same Americans who have discriminated against us? These weighty ruminations comprise the philosophical underpinnings for Ellison's assertion of blacks as American patriots—as defenders and advocates of the nation's cause. For all the ambivalence of motivation it reveals, it leaves little doubt about the need to affirm the principles of democracy. Invisible Man does not entertain the possibility of anything other than America. He rejects Ras's black nationalism, rejects any alternative that does not include affirming the values of the nation's founding. This is one lesson he did not learn from Leroy.

It is a testament to Ellison's philosophical adroitness that he has somehow enlisted Leroy's proto–Third World politics in fashioning Invisible Man's American democratic appeal. Those who see political opportunism in this transformation, however, miss the broader context of Ellison's intellectual development in this period. In the years following World War II Ellison's patriotic sensibilities expanded, albeit with a necessary reserve, to allow a distance of critique. *Invisible Man*, therefore, is best read as an assertion rather than a renunciation. That said, it is hard not to wonder how *Invisible Man* might have been received had Ellison retained more of Leroy's journal in the published book. Raymond A. Mazurek speculated on this as well, writing that the reasons Ellison eliminated Leroy are among the most "intriguing unanswered questions" about the novel. "Had more of Leroy's journal survived," he writes, "Ellison probably would have been read as a champion of the truncated anticommunist left in the McCarthy years."

But even though Ellison's decision to remove Leroy may seem unclear on the level of idea, on the level of craft, it is obvious. Without Leroy's journal to give him an ideological compass, Invisible Man is left to find his own stumbling way toward the illumination and insight of the epilogue. The result is a character as deeply flawed and surprisingly heroic as all human beings are capable of becoming when faced with challenge.[30]

Leroy, the name if not the character, lived on in Ellison's mind to the end. The manuscripts of Ellison's second novel include at least two Leroys, one of whom plays a primary role in one of the most rollicking incidents Ellison would compose. This second Leroy serves a similar function that *Invisible Man*'s did, compelling the protagonist to action, forcing him to confront the unresolved challenges before him. The second Leroy appears as Alonzo Hickman is walking through Washington, D.C., in search of an acquaintance who might lead him to Sunraider. Just as Hickman passes an old barbershop, familiar from his days touring the city as a jazz musician, he notices a man rushing toward him from the shop with a white neckcloth snapping in the breeze. The next thing he knows, the small man has picked him up from the knees and hoisted him in the air. After he is lowered back to the ground, he notices that the little man suffers from a disfiguring skin condition, something like vitiligo, that has left his face a patchwork of color—"red, white, and blueblack!" Trying to disguise his surprise, Hickman asks what the man wants, soon discovering that it is a case of mistaken identity. The little man, whom Hickman soon learns is named Leroy, refuses to believe that Hickman is anyone other than an underground revolutionary leader by the name of "Chief Sam the Fucking Liberator!"

The most striking thing about this episode is Leroy's extensive recapitulation of a speech that Chief Sam supposedly gave before a white judge as he was being charged with rape. Leroy is seeking absolution from Hickman for perceived weakness or loss of faith. In his notes for the novel Ellison admits to himself the contrivance of this scene, making a striking comparison in the process. "Think of Leroy's rant and Bigger's scene with Mrs. Dalton and Mary: [It's] as off base as that scene in that chief wouldn't have had a chance to make his speech. 'Contrivance' is the term." It is striking that *Native Son* was on his mind at such a time, particularly given Ellison's public distancing of himself in relation to Wright as far as their fiction was concerned. Although Ellison was often generous in print about Wright's importance to him on a personal level, he would never admit any debt to Wright when it came to his mature fiction. Though this is but a small moment, it nonetheless suggests that Ellison's mind was alive to the potential resonance between his fiction and Wright's.[31]

Leroy tells of how he had a revelation in which "Chief" appeared to him and showed him the error of his ways. It was then that he wished he had not played the role he did (reading Chief's "confession") in Chief's conviction. This Chief, it seems, is a self-styled race leader who acts through the subterranean power of race magic, challenging the white man with his very own terms, even going so far as to challenge "rape." ("I keep hearing it [rape] and I ask myself how can it *be* that it's all these things for you folks and only one for me?") Finally Ivey, the barber, comes out of the shop to get Leroy. He explains to Hickman that Leroy does this every time the moon is full, accosting any well-dressed dark-skinned black man he sees, claiming that he is Chief Sam, someone whom he'd only heard tell about from his grandfather. Leroy is "crazy" and yet speaks truth, if in a convoluted form.

The material relating to Hickman's encounter with Leroy is among the most revised in all the computer files, with twenty-five partial and complete variants of the episode. Hickman's encounter with Leroy and the other incidents along his journey seem to share a common purpose. They all concern identity: reminding Hickman of his past, mistaking him for someone else, or challenging him with his present predicament. But even though these encounters bear a kind of internal narrative logic, they seem at quite a distance from the putative goal of the fiction—namely, to explore Hickman's relationship with Bliss/Sunraider. In that regard, these scenes seem like little more than diverting distractions.

In an undated note Ellison sheds light on the purpose of the episode. "It seems that Leroy is telling Hickman about an initiation ritual in which the figure in his dark room is conducting. Thus the seven questions—or mistakes—have to do with a riddle. But in the street scene Leroy is putting *Hickman* through an initiation in which Leroy and his fantasies constitute the riddle. That riddle points to politics and thus to the complex meaning which lies in Hickman's relationship with Sunraider. What is the secret knowledge which underlies all this craziness?" What reads like a scene improvised on the fly is actually highly structured, even labored. And although Ellison asserts confidently that the "riddle points to politics" and the "complex meaning" in Hickman's relationship with Sunraider, the "secret knowledge" the riddle guards is unknown, even to Ellison. It is this lack of certainty that leads to the overarching sense of directionlessness. The underlying connections to the novel's chief theme are clearly in place, but they are not yet activated in the plot. The result is a missed fictive opportunity, dissipating rather than intensifying narrative momentum.[32]

Ellison's second Leroy is in many ways as indispensable and enigmatic as his first. As creators of chaos, they challenge both of Ellison's protagonists to find order in their experiences. As unabsorbed and perhaps unabsorbable elements of their respective fictions, they reveal Ellison's novels in the very process of becoming.

Conclusion

2010

The story of Ellison's unfinished second novel is most often told in tones of tragedy. "The tragedy," Stanley Crouch asserts, "lies in the weight Ralph put on himself. He created this grand tower in his mind, with a priceless penthouse at the top, which was virtually impossible to climb." Speaking to Ellison's biographer Arnold Rampersad a decade after Ellison's death, Toni Morrison offered a more nuanced interpretation of Ellison's literary career. She noted his grand achievements and continued esteem. "And yet one is tempted to say also that it is tinged with tragedy, because expectations of much more fictional work were never realized. But tragedy is not the right word; it requires grandeur. The better word is melancholy." For Morrison, that melancholy took the shape of Ellison's disconnection from "the contemporary world of late twentieth-century African Americans." Ellison, in other words, was a man out of phase with his time. "I don't think Ellison ever saw the need to revisit or redress anything he had done or not done," Morrison continues, "or to challenge his obvious level of success with more demanding ones. He saw himself as a black literary patrician, but at some level this was a delusion. It was simply his solution to that persistent problem black writers are confronted with: art and, or versus, identity. I don't see tragedy in his predicament. I see a kind of sadness instead."[1]

Such characterizations portray Ellison as a man beset by circumstances he himself had created and burdened by a particular perspective on a nation and a history that remained forever beyond his grasp. His failure, such accounts seem to suggest, was not only artistic but personal: he simply could not muster the fortitude to respond to the challenges of his art.

The greatest challenge he set for himself was, of course, his manuscript in progress. Ellison took on the seemingly impossible task of rendering in fiction the American experience in the second half of the twentieth century. "At its best, fiction allows for a summing up," Ellison explained to John Hersey in a 1974 interview. "The fiction writer abstracts from the flow of experience certain abiding patterns, and projects those patterns as they affect the lives and consciousness of the characters. So fiction allows for a summing up. It allows for contemplation of the moral significance of human events. . . . In any case, it is that aura of summing up, that pause for contemplation of the moral significance of the history we've been through, that I have been reaching for, in my work on this new book." This philosophy separates the second novel from *Invisible Man,* which concerned itself not within summing up, but rather with projecting possibility, with articulating a singular voice with the power to speak for others. The aura of summing up, a redolent phrase, embodies a sense of collective values and identity. It asks the novelist to bear responsibility for both the literary and the sociopolitical implications of his craft. This fusion of art and politics is at the center of Ellison's artistic vision. It may also offer the best explanation of the novel's incompletion.[2]

It has become something of a critical fashion, both during the last decades of Ellison's life and in the years since his
death, to diagnose the causes of what many perceived as Ellison's signal failure. Perhaps the fire in 1967 that burned up a
significant portion of the novel was ultimately too much
psychologically for Ellison to bear. Perhaps the series of political assassinations in the 1960s—Malcolm, Martin, Medgar,
the Kennedys—cooled him to the concept of a novel centered
around a shooting on the floor of the Senate. These suggestions, while eminently reasonable, prove insufficient. They
fail to consider Ellison's own explanation of the novel's protracted composition. In Ellison's words it is possible to hear
the tones not of defeat or exhaustion but, rather, of aspiration
and promise—the search for a response fitting to the great
challenge of his call—the aura of summing up.

The danger in all of these various theories and interpretations of the second novel's incompletion is that they risk dis-
tracting our critical attention from the one thing we know for
certain: that Ellison wrote thousands of pages, much of which
is of fine quality and all of which evidences Ellison's activity
during the last decades of his life. Granted, critics offering
views of the second novel have based their interpretations
largely on *Juneteenth* rather than on *Three Days Before the
Shooting.* . . . With that in mind, it is clear what a critic like
Norman Podhoretz means when claims in his 1999 essay
"What Happened to Ralph Ellison" that, "in the case of *Juneteenth*, the ghost haunting the prose is not Hemingway, however, but Faulkner." He continues:

> Other parts of the 2,000-page manuscript he left
> behind may prove me wrong, but for now my spec-
> ulation is that Ellison—a man of great intelligence
> and literary erudition who had an ear second to

none—knew that Faulkner had invaded and taken him over and that this was why he could never finish his book. I can imagine him struggling for 40 years to get Faulkner's sound out of his head; I can imagine him searching desperately for the lost voice he had created in *Invisible Man;* I can imagine him trying to fool himself into thinking that he had finally found it again, and then realizing he had not; and I can imagine him being reduced to despair at this literary enslavement into which some incorrigible defect in his nature had sold him—and to a Southern master, at that!

The range of manuscripts published in *Three Days Before the Shooting. . .* provide those "other parts" that Podhoretz wondered about. Although Ellison's debts to Faulkner are obvious in the portions of the manuscript published as *Juneteenth,* they are not all-consuming as Podhoretz feared. Ellison's was not a struggle to get Faulkner out of his head; it was not even the search for a lost voice. Instead, it was the search for a form that could encompass the audacious aim expressed in the "aura of summing up," a way of imaginatively projecting a nation on the page. The novel as it takes shape on Ellison's computer could not be further from Faulkner in style and intention. Instead, it returns to the freewheeling spirit familiar from *Invisible Man* with its emphasis on incident and raucous humor. And even though what Ellison wrote on the computer is not nearly as fully achieved in its style and execution as the typescripts, it shows an author still very much of his own mind and style, not in the thrall of some great white master.[3]

What makes Ellison's work during the 1980s and 1990s so crucial is that it doggedly affirms the broadness of Ellison's aim and the incompletion of his experiment. *Juneteenth*'s honed, Faulknerian prose is in some ways deceiving; its polish belies the unfinished struggle Ellison was even then undergoing on the level of form and theme. Perhaps his knowledge of this fact restrained him from publishing material that seems to meet and exceed the standards of past fiction, at least on the level of style. Ellison kept going, continuing to complicate his themes, even as he seemed to take backward steps in style. As readers it would be a grave error to discount the work Ellison did in his last decade simply because the quality of its prose does not match that of the 1970s typescripts. Without Ellison's computer files, something profoundly humanizing would be lost from his manuscript. For all their flaws, they remind us of the rich characterization and deep humor of which Ellison was capable. They recall the picaresque adventure for which he was known. They proffer the kinds of characters—iconic yet vernacular—that are the hallmark of *Invisible Man*. Most important, they connect to Ellison's earliest vision of the novel as it took shape in his memories of Oklahoma. To overlook them is to do a grave disservice to Ellison's literary legacy. To read them is to witness a new novel in the making.

Ralph Ellison's second novel may never escape the singular mystery of its failed publication. If so, then we will have overlooked one of the most provocative, stymieing, and exhilarating literary artifacts of the twentieth century. Just months before his death, Ellison affirmed his familiar certainty that he would see his second novel through to publication. At the same time, he expressed another sentiment, a minor chord to contrast with the major chord of his assuredness: something like hope. Both of these sentiments are apparent in Ellison's words to David Remnick in the last interview Ellison would give before his death. "When you are younger," he explains, "you are so eager to be published, I am eager to publish this book. That's why I stay here, and not in the country. I'm eager to finish it and see how it turns out." Even after forty years of writing, Ellison was animated by the possibilities of his fiction, by the promise of discovery that awaited him with the next scene, the next turn of phrase.[4]

On December 30, 1993, Ellison saved to his computer the last file he would compose related to his second novel. In the weeks before his death, he told friends that the book was nearly finished. The textual evidence now proves otherwise. Whether this was evidence of an old man's self-deception or of a wily trickster having one last laugh, or both, is unclear. This much, however, is certain: when he died in April 1994, he left behind no instructions on how the novel should be handled, no Nabokovian injunctions that the book be burned, no complete table of contents, not even a definitive title. Instead, he left a brilliant mess of a book, at times as difficult to read as it is to ignore.

The very things that make Ellison's second novel imperfect are also what make it such a compelling metaphor for America. Protean, unfinished, grand in vision but often flawed in execution, marked by failures and triumphs, it reflects the complexities of American life in a way that a finished novel could not. Precisely because of these conflicting qualities, it might just be worth considering as this century's first candidate for the Great American Novel. An idea born of the nineteenth century, the Great American Novel is now reduced to a hoary conceit. But the term finds new life when applied to a work such as Ellison's manuscript in progress.

Like the nation itself, Ellison's second novel is a big, cumbersome, divided crazy quilt of voices and ideas. The challenge for the reader, like the challenge for the citizen, is to imagine unity out of seemingly irreconcilable diversity. At its center, it offers a fundamental test of American democratic practice and a call to account for democratic principle. It asks us to recognize promise—of the novel, of the Republic—in the face of pessimism. Its greatness lies in the insight it offers into American life and in the discrete moments that reveal Ellison as a writer with much wisdom to impart concerning the state of our union. The only partly realized promise of its greatness sheds light on Ellison's genius as well as on the challenges of race and identity that remain America's signal preoccupations. Like the nation he loved and the novel he would never finish, Ralph Ellison, too, was in progress to the last.

Notes

Introduction

1. Ellison, *Invisible Man*, 7.
2. McKay, *Harlem Glory*, 14.
3. Ellison, *Invisible Man*, 8.
4. Graham and Singh, eds., *Conversations*, 279.
5. Galenson, *Old Masters and Young Geniuses*, 4.
6. Ellison, *Invisible Man*, 581.
7. Ellison, *Invisible Man*, xx, xx–xxi.
8. Ellison, *Collected Essays*, 820–21.
9. Graham and Singh, eds., *Conversations*, 385–86.
10. See "Study and Experience: An Interview with Ralph Ellison," Robert B. Stepto and Michael S. Harper (1976) and "Visible Man," David Remnick (1994), both in Graham and Singh, eds., *Conversations*, for two such instances.
11. Watts, *Heroism and the Black Intellectual*, 32.
12. Ellison, *Juneteenth*, 366.

Chapter One

1982

1. Ellison's financial records show that he purchased an Osborne I on January 8, 1982 (in addition to another for his wife, Fanny, on September 30

of that year); an Osborne Executive on October 11, 1983; and an IBM on January 7, 1988. The Osborne I, introduced in April 1981, was the first truly portable personal computer commercially available in the United States. After strong initial sales, Osborne ran into financial difficulties, filing for bankruptcy in September 1983.

2. Graham and Singh, eds., *Conversations*, 381–82.

3. Graham and Singh, eds., *Conversations*, 381–82.

4. Graham and Singh, eds., *Conversations*, 383.

5. For a fascinating discussion of "fluid texts" and the art of fiction on the computer during this period of transformation in the 1980s, see Catano, "Computer-Based Writing."

6. DeSantis and Callahan, "Some Cord of Kinship," 609, 610.

7. DeSantis and Callahan, "Some Cord of Kinship," 610.

8. Callahan, "Making of Ralph Ellison's *Juneteenth*." Keep in mind that these distinctions are critical interventions, meant to assist the reader in coming to terms with the sheer magnitude of Ellison's text. They are artificial in that Ellison did not experience his compositional process in discrete phases, but they are nonetheless grounded in the details of the novel's protracted compositional history, reflecting profound shifts in Ellison's approach to the text.

9. For a fine exploration of the intersection between the computer and the novel, see Fitzpatrick, "Exhaustion of Literature." Fitzpatrick argues against the extreme positions of textual protectionists and technophiles, asserting that "where computers and novels come into contact, the result need not be conflict; instead, the relationship could prove symbiotic" (520).

10. Baer, ed., *Conversations with Derek Walcott*, 105.

11. Podhoretz, "What Happened to Ralph Ellison," 55.

12. Graham and Singh, eds., *Conversations*, 218.

13. Winter, "It's All in My Head."

14. DeSantis and Callahan, "Some Cord of Kinship," 609.

15. On an envelope dated January 9, 1985, Ellison has scrawled the following complaint: "Osborne. I'm writing this on an EXECUTIVE computer and an IBM Quiet printer that am so ignorant of the how to patch the damn thing that I'm wasting a good part of my investment" (Ralph Ellison Archive, Library of Congress, box 138, folder 3).

16. Robert J. Sawyer's web site is: www.sfwriter. com. De Santis and Callahan, "Some Cord of Kinship," 611.

17. Ellison only occasionally dated his numerous drafts, but Fanny Ellison was far more diligent in this regard. The revised typescript to Book II includes a note in Mrs. Ellison's hand stating that Ellison had taken the material to Plainfield to revise it during the summer of 1986.

18. One significant exception to this discarding is Ellison's work on what was Chapter XII from Book I in the last months of 1993. That December 30, Ellison saved his last known file to the computer—"Rockmore," which offers a first-person account in McIntyre's voice of the strange developments at Jessie Rockmore's estate. It is unclear why Ellison would have turned to this material given that he seems previously to have neglected it for nearly a decade.

In regard to *Juneteenth,* John Callahan asserts a similar conclusion when he recalls his own realization that the Ellison of the computers was not necessarily a more mature novelist than he was decades before, that "the Ellison writing in the '60s and '70s was as mature as any novelist needs to be" (De Santis and Callahan, "Some Cord of Kinship," 611).

19. Ellison, *Collected Essays,* 266. Ellington, "Race for Space," 293.

20. Ellison Archive, box 138, folder 5, and box 139, folder 6.

21. Callahan, *Juneteenth,* xxvii.

22. Ellison, *Collected Essays,* 52.

23. Updike, "Late Works."

24. Indeed, as Wershler-Henry points out in *The Iron Whim,* "Typewriting comes into being at the same time as the notion of public authorship, aiding and abetting it" (97).

25. Graham and Singh, eds., *Conversations,* 70.

Chapter Two

1970

1. Kaiser, "Critical Look at Ellison's Fiction," 95.

2. Mason, "Ralph Ellison and the Underground Man," 21. Watts, *Heroism and the Black Intellectual,* 31.

3. McPherson, "Indivisible Man," 55.

4. Baraka and Neal, *Black Fire,* 652.

5. Warren, *Who Speaks for the Negro?* 346.

6. The full text of Johnson's speech is available online at the Lyndon B. Johnson Presidential Library, University of Texas: http://www.lbjlib.utexas.edu/johnson/archives.hom/speeches.hom/650604.asp.

7. Richard M. Nixon, Annual Message to the Congress on the State of the Union, January 22, 1970. Daniel Moynihan's memo available at: http://www.questia.com/PM.qst?a=o&se=gglsc&d=5001864516.

8. Ellison to Morteza Sprague, May 18, 1954. Ralph Ellison Archive, Library of Congress, box 68, folder 3.

9. Ellison Archive, box 108, folder 5.

10. Ellison Archive, box 108, folder 5.

11. Ellison Archive, box 108, folder 5.

12. Ellison, *Collected Essays,* 581.

13. Ellison, *Collected Essays,* 587.

14. Ellison, *Collected Essays,* 587, 588.

15. Ellison Archive, box 108, folder 6.

16. Ellison Archive, box 108, folder 6.

17. "Black America 1970."

18. Mason, "Native Son Strikes Home."

19. Ellison Archive, box 110, folder 22.

20. Rampersad, *Ellison,* 438.

21. Undated note on stationary labeled "From the desk of Ralph Ellison," Ellison Archive, box 138, folder 5.

22. Graham and Singh, eds., *Conversations,* 409; Watts, *Heroism and the Black Intellectual,* 48; Ellison Archive, box 102, folder 5.

23. Warren, *Who Speaks for the Negro?* 339. Allen, *Strangers among Us,* 30.

24. Ellison, *Collected Essays,* 820–21.

25. Ellison Archive, box 177, folder 2, fols. 50–51, 54.

26. Ellison letter to *Time* quoted in Graham and Singh, eds., *Conversations,* 65.

27. Lott, *Disappearing Liberal Intellectual,* 67.

28. Forrest, "Conversation with Ralph Ellison," 29.

28. Ellison Archive, box 140, folder 2.

Chapter Three

1955

1. Ralph Ellison Archive, Library of Congress, box 68, folder 3.

2. Ellison's notes reveal that he was considering other possible dates, including this rather specific one from an undated, handwritten note: "On the day of April, 1953 a chartered airplane load of elderly Southern Negroes put down at the . . . ." Ellison Archive, box 140, folder 4. Graham and Singh, eds., *Conversations,* 147.

3. Rampersad, *Ellison,* 226.

4. Eddy, *Rites of Identity,* 112.

5. Ellison, *Collected Essays,* 187–88.

6. Graham and Singh, eds., *Conversations,* 101.

7. Ellison Archive, box 138, folder 2.

8. Graham and Singh, eds., *Conversations*, 97.

9. Watts, *Heroism and the Black Intellectual*, 81, 108. The title of the unpublished essay comes from a series of notes Ellison labeled as "The American Language as Symbolic Agency," Ellison Archive, box 95, folder 15. Rampersad, *Ellison*, 549.

10. West, *Democracy Matters*, 103.

11. Ellison Archive, box 40, folder 4.

12. Ellison Archive, box 140, folder 4. Ellison, *Collected Essays*, 129.

13. This note is taken from Ellison's computer discs and is not yet filed in print form in the Ellison Archive. Singh, *Black Is a Country*, 7.

14. Ellison Archive, box 68, folder 3.

15. Wright, "Foreword."

16. Ellison, *Collected Essays*, 31–32.

17. Warren, *Who Speaks for the Negro?* 339.

18. Martin Luther King, Jr., "The American Dream," in King, *Testament of Hope*, 209. In King's last years, however, as the movement's progress slowed and struggles for black freedom moved from the courts to the less governable provinces of American life, he seemed to see the limitations of patriotic appeal.

19. Douglass, *Selected Speeches and Writings*, 191.

20. Douglass, *Selected Speeches and Writings*, 191.

21. Douglass, *Selected Speeches and Writings*, 195.

22. Ellison, *Collected Essays*, 323, 324–25.

23. Graham and Singh, eds., *Conversations*, 96.

24. "Bliss's Birth," Ellison Archive, box 119, folder 9. Ellison Archive, box 141, folder 5.

25. "Bliss's Birth," Ellison Archive, box 119, folder 9.

26. "Hickman in Washington, D.C.," forthcoming in *Three Days Before the Shooting . . . .*

Chapter Four

1952

1. This notebook is filed among the *Invisible Man* notes, not the Hickman manuscripts, in the Ralph Ellison Archive, Library of Congress, box 152, folder 6.

2. Ellison, *Collected Essays*, 278; Callahan, ed., *Trading Twelves*, 94.

3. See Rampersad's account of *Invisible Man*'s textual genesis in *Ellison*, 193–96.

4. Callahan, ed., *Trading Twelves*, 16, 21.

5. Jackson, "Birth of the Critic."

6. Ralph Ellison Archive, Library of Congress, box 148, folder 6.

7. "Harvard's Rallying Cry." Goodheart, "I Love My Vincent Baby," 88.

8. The eponymous Rinehart passed away at the age of seventy-seven the year after *Invisible Man*'s publication. It is unclear whether he was aware of his immortalization in Ellison's fiction, though he was certainly familiar with Frazier's song. Ellison, *Collected Essays*, 223.

9. De Santis and Callahan, "Some Cord of Kinship." Ellison offers his own definition of Bliss through Hickman in "Bliss's Birth": "I thought, *I'll call him Bliss, because they say that's what ignorance is.* Yes, and little did I realize that it was the name of the old heathen life I had already lost" (332). Ellison, *Collected Essays*, 223. Ellison, *Invisible Man*, 498.

10. Of course, one should not read too much into this, given that Ellison was a casual speller at best and wont to experiment with different spellings for many of his characters' names: Leroy and LeRoy; Millsap and Millsaps; Cleophus, Cliophus, and Cliofus.

11. Ellison, *Invisible Man*, 494.

12. Ellison, *Collected Essays*, 110, 511.

13. Ellison Archive, box 141, folder 5.

14. Ellison Archive, box 140, folder 6.

15. The three-book rumor likely originated with Ellison's following statement from James Alan McPherson's 1970 profile of Ellison, "Indivisible Man": "If I find that it is better to make it a three section book, to issue it in three volumes, I would do that as long as I thought that each volume had a compelling interest in itself." However, on August 3, 1986, the *New York Times* ran a brief piece entitled "In His Own Good Time" alongside John Edgar Wideman's review of *Going to the Territory* in which Ellison unequivocally dismisses rumors of a multivolume publication. "No, it's not," he responds, "I know that's gotten around, though."

16. "Bliss's Birth," 321.

17. A handwritten note on an envelope dated April 1, 1986, includes a table of contents for one of Ellison's computer disks, txt 5. "Bliss.nts / Esquire / Esquire / Laura / Laughter / Leroy / Rhineheart / Severen/."

18. In the one of the few remaining notes in which Ellison refers to Bliss by his full name, he seems to make this precise point. "Bliss Proteus Rhinehart returned to his part very much as a man to his mother or a dog to his vomit. . ." Undated notes, Hickman Manuscripts, Ellison Archive, box 140, folder 6.

19. Ellison Archive, box 152, folder 6.

20. Ellison Archive, box 140, folder 6.

Chapter Five

1950

1. Ralph Ellison Archive, Library of Congress, box 152, folder 2.

2. Ellison, *Collected Essays,* 221.

3. Tate, "Notes on the Invisible Women," 254–55.

4. Smethurst, "'Something Warmly, Infuriatingly Feminine,'" 138. Hill, "Visual Art of *Invisible Man.*"

5. Ellison, *Invisible Man,* 6.

6. Ellison Archive, box 147, folder 1.

7. Waniek, "Space Where Sex Should Be." Baldwin, *Price of the Ticket,* 273.

8. Ellison Archive, box 172.

9. Ellison, *Collected Essays,* 147–48.

10. Smethurst, "'Something Warmly, Infuriatingly Feminine,'"119.

11. Ellison Archive, box 144, folder 6. Hill and Hill, *Ellison's "Invisible Man,"* 47.

12. Ellison Archive, box 142, folders 2, 9, 3.

13. Wright, *Native Son,* 501.

14. Book I typescript, Ellison Archive, box 132, folder 2, 142, 143.

15. Ellison, *Invisible Man,* 452.

16. Callahan, *In the African-American Grain,* 170.

17. Book I typescript, Ellison Archive, box 132, folder 2, 143.

18. Book I typescript, Ellison Archive, box 132, folder 2, 196.

Chapter Six

1945

1. Ralph Ellison, *'48: The Magazine of the Year* (Walter Ross), March 1, 1948, Ralph Ellison Archive, Library of Congress.

2. Graham and Singh, eds., *Conversations,* 4.

3. Rampersad, *Ellison,* 197.

4. Jackson, *Ellison: Emergence of Genius,* 336.

5. Perhaps it should come as little surprise that Ellison would retain

this kind of consistency of practice and thought throughout his literary career. Ellison displays this same intellectual integrity in other areas of his intellectual life. Arnold Rampersad remarks in his biography of Ellison that Ellison's emerging views on color and culture are apparent even in his college term papers. "His views in 1936, expressed in his course essays, are surprisingly, even astonishingly, consistent with the core views on culture he would expound in his maturity. Even in 1936, he disliked the idea that separate races existed with distinctly separate endowments, but believed instead in the fertility of culture and the dynamic of cross-cultural exchange" (Rampersad, *Ellison*, 78).

6. Ellison, *Collected Essays*, 391.

7. Graham and Singh, eds., *Conversations*, 217.

8. Warren, *So Black and Blue*, 23.

9. Graham and Singh, eds., *Conversations*, 17.

10. Ralph Ellison Archive, Library of Congress, box 102, folder 5.

11. Ellison, *Invisible Man*, 571.

12. Jackson, *Ellison: Emergence of Genius*, 414.

13. For examples, see Brennan, "Ellison and Ellison"; Baker, "Failed Prophet and Falling Stock"; and Schaub, "From Ranter to Writer." Foley, "Rhetoric of Anticommunism in Invisible Man."

14. Ellison Archive, box 151, folder 6.

15. Morel, *Ellison and the Raft of Hope*, 77. Ellison, *Collected Essays*, 151, 154.

16. Ellison, *Invisible Man*, xx–xxi.

17. Mazurek, "Writer on the Left."

18. Rampersad, *Ellison*, 242.

19. Ellison Archive, box 145, folder 6.

20. Ellison Archive, box 145, folder 6. Invisible Man does not push back against Leroy's statement, or even comment on it, except in one draft where Ellison has penciled the following in the margins by way of Invisible Man's response: "Nuts, I thought, nuts! What about invisibility? What if they don't even see you?" (box 145, folder 6). This halting objection to Leroy's assertion of cosmopolitan identity gets no further development, however.

21. Ellison, *Invisible Man*, 579; Ellison Archive, box 145, folder 6.

22. Ellison, *Invisible Man*, 579; Ellison Archive, box 145, folder 6.

23. Ellison Archive, box 152, folder 3.

24. Ellison Archive, box 151, folder 9.

25. Ellison Archive, box 142, folder 2.

26. Ellison Archive, box 142, folder 3.

27. Ellison Archive, box 152, folder 3.

28. Ellison Archive, box 147, folder 4.
29. Ellison Archive, box 140, folder 10.
30. Mazurek, "Writer on the Left," 3.
31. Ellison Archive, box 138, folder 4.
32. Ellison Archive, box 140, folder 2.

Conclusion

2010

1. Rampersad, *Ellison,* 551, 549–50.
2. Ellison, *Collected Essays,* 820–21.
3. Podhoretz, "What Happened to Ralph Ellison," 55–56.
4. Graham and Singh, eds., *Conversations,* 395.

Bibliography

Allen, Danielle S. *Strangers among Us: Anxieties of Citizenship since Brown v. Board of Education*. Chicago: University of Chicago Press, 2004.

Baer, William, ed. *Conversations with Derek Walcott*. Jackson: University of Mississippi Press, 1996.

Baker, Houston, Jr. *Blues, Ideology, and Afro-American Literature: A Vernacular Theory*. Chicago: University of Chicago Press, 1984.

———. "Failed Prophet and Falling Stock: Why Ralph Ellison Was Never Avant-Garde." *Stanford Humanities Review* 1 (1999): 4–11.

———. "To Move without Moving: An Analysis of Creativity and Commerce in Ralph Ellison's Trueblood Episode." *PMLA* 98 (1983): 828–45.

Baldwin, James. *The Price of the Ticket: Collected Nonfiction, 1948–1985*. New York: St. Martin's, 1985.

Baraka, Amiri, and Larry Neal. *Black Fire: An Anthology of Afro-American Writing*. 1968. Reprint, Washington, D.C.: Black Classic Press, 2007.

Bentson, Kimberly W., ed. *Speaking for You: The Vision of Ralph Ellison*. Washington, D.C.: Howard University Press, 1990.

"Black America 1970." *Time*, April 6, 1970, 13.

Brennan, Timothy. "Ellison and Ellison: The Solipsism of *Invisible Man*." *CLA Journal* 25 (December 1981): 162–81.

Burke, Kenneth. *A Grammar of Motives*. 1945. Reprint, Berkeley: University of California Press, 1969.

———. *The Philosophy of Literary Form*. 1941. Reprint, Baton Rouge: Louisiana State University Press, 1967.

———. *Rhetoric of Motives*. Berkeley: University of California Press, 1969.

Butler, Robert J. *The Critical Response to Ralph Ellison*. Westport, Conn.: Greenwood Press, 2000.

Callahan, John F. *In the African-American Grain: Call-and-Response in Twentieth-Century Black Fiction*. Middletown, Conn.: Wesleyan University Press, 1978.

Callahan, John F., ed. *Ralph Ellison's "Invisible Man": A Casebook*. New York: Oxford University Press, 2004.

———. "The Making of Ralph Ellison's *Juneteenth*." Paper presented at the Literary Fact and Historical Fiction Symposium, Middlebury College, Middlebury, Vt., March 3, 2000.

———. *Trading Twelves: The Selected Letters of Ralph Ellison and Albert Murray.*. New York: Modern Library, 2000.

Catano, James V. "Computer-Based Writing: Navigating the Fluid Text." *College Composition and Communication* 36 (1985): 309–16.

Covo, Jacqueline. *The Blinking Eye: Ralph Waldo Ellison and His American, French, German and Italian Critics, 1952–1971*. Metuchen, N.J.: Scarecrow, 1974.

De Santis, Christopher C., and John F. Callahan. "'Some Cord of Kinship Stronger and Deeper than Blood': An Interview with John F. Callahan, Editor of Ralph Ellison's *Invisible Man*." *African American Review* 34 (2000): 601–20.

Douglass, Frederick. *Narrative of the Life of Frederick Douglass, an American Slave; Written by Himself*. 1845. Reprint, New York: Penguin, 1982.

———. *Frederick Douglass: Selected Speeches and Writings*. Edited by Philip S. Foner and Yuval Taylor. New York: Lawrence Hill Books, 2000.

Drake, St. Clair, and Horace R. Cayton. *Black Metropolis: A Study of Negro Life in a Northern City*. New York: Harcourt, Brace, 1945.

Eddy, Beth. *The Rites of Identity: The Religious Naturalism and Cultural Criticism of Kenneth Burke and Ralph Ellison*. Princeton, N.J.: Princeton University Press, 2003.

Ellington, Duke. "The Race for Space." Ca. 1959. Reprinted in Mark Tucker, ed., *The Duke Ellington Reader*. New York: Oxford University Press, 1995.

Ellison, Ralph. "Backwacking: A Plea to the Senator." *Massachusetts Review* 18 (1977): 411–16.

———. *The Collected Essays of Ralph Ellison*. Edited by John F. Callahan. New York: Modern Library, 1995.

———. "And Hickman Arrives." *Noble Savage* 1 (1960): 5–49.

———. *Invisible Man*. New York: Random House, 1952.

———. *Invisible Man*. Edited by John F. Callahan. New York: Random House, 1999.

———. "It Always Breaks Out." *Partisan Review* 30 (Spring 1963): 13–28.

———. "Juneteenth." *Quarterly Review of Literature* 4 (1965): 262–76.

———. *Juneteenth: A Novel.* Edited by John Callahan. New York: Random House, 1999.

———. "Night-Talk." *Quarterly Review of Literature* 16 (1969): 317–29.

———. "Out of the Hospital and under the Bar." In *Soon, One Morning,* edited by Herbert Hill, 242–90. New York: Alfred A. Knopf, 1963.

———. "The Roof, the Steeple and the People." *Quarterly Review of Literature* 10 (1960): 115–28.

———. "A Song of Innocence." *Iowa Review* 1 (Spring 1970): 30–40.

———. *Three Days Before the Shooting. . . : The Unfinished Second Novel.* Edited by John Callahan and Adam Bradley. New York: Random House, 2010.

Faulkner, William. "On Privacy: The American Dream." *Harper's,* July 1955, 33–38.

Fitzpatrick, Kathleen. "The Exhaustion of Literature: Novels, Computers, and the Threat of Obsolescence." *Contemporary Literature* 43 (2002): 518–59.

Foley, Barbara. "From Communism to Brotherhood: The Drafts of *Invisible Man.*" In *Left of the Color Line: Race, Radicalism, and Twentieth-Century Literature of the United States,* edited by Bill V. Mullen and James Smethurst, 163–82. Chapel Hill: University of North Carolina Press, 2003.

———. "Ralph Ellison as Proletarian Journalist." *Science and Society* 62 (1997): 537–56..

———. "Reading Redness: Politics and Audience in Ralph Ellison's Early Short Stories." *JNT: Journal of Narrative Theory* 29 (1999): 323–39.

———. "The Rhetoric of Anticommunism in Invisible Man." *College English* 59 (1977): 530–47.

Forrest, Leon. "A Conversation with Ralph Ellison." *Muhammed Speaks,* December 15, 1972, 29–31.

Gates, Henry Louis, Jr. *The Signifying Monkey: A Theory of African-American Literary Criticism.* New York: Oxford University Press, 1988.

Goodheart, Adam. "I Love My Vincent Baby . . . ." *Harvard Magazine,* September–October 2002, 88.

Graham, Maryemma, and Amritjit Singh, eds. *Conversations with Ralph Ellison.* Jackson: University of Mississippi Press, 1995.

Harper, Michael S. *Chant of Saints: A Gathering of Afro-American Literature, Art, and Scholarship.* Chicago: University of Illinois Press, 1979.

"Harvard's Rallying Cry." *Western Folklore* vol. 12, no. 2 (1953): 139–40.

Hill, Herbert, ed. *Soon, One Morning.* New York: Alfred A. Knopf, 1963.

Hill, Lena M. "The Visual Art of *Invisible Man:* Ellison's Portrait of Blackness." Forthcoming in *American Literature,* 2010.

Hill, Michael D., and Lena M. Hill. *Ralph Ellison's "Invisible Man": A Reference Guide.* Westport, Conn.: Greenwood, 2008.

Jackson, Lawrence P. "The Birth of the Critic: The Literary Friendship of Ralph Ellison and Richard Wright." *American Literature* 72 (2000): 321–35.

———. *Ralph Ellison: Emergence of Genius.* New York: John Wiley and Sons, 2002.

Kaiser, Ernest. "A Critical Look at Ellison's Fiction and at Social and Literary Criticism by and about the Author." *Black World,* 53–59, 81–97.

King, Martin Luther, Jr. *A Testament of Hope: The Essential Writings and Speeches of Martin Luther King, Jr.,* edited by James M. Washington. New York: Harper, 1986.

Kouwenhoven, John A. *The Beer Can by the Highway: Essays on What's American about America.* 1961. Reprint, Baltimore: Johns Hopkins University Press, 1988.

Lott, Eric. *The Disappearing Liberal Intellectual.* New York: Basic Books, 2007.

Mason, Clifford. "Native Son Strikes Home." *Life,* May 8, 1970.

———. "Ralph Ellison and the Underground Man." *Black World,* December 1970, 20–26.

Mazurek, Raymond A. "Reinventing Ralph Ellison." *College Literature* 32, no. 2 (2005): 170–76.

———. "Writer on the Left: Class and Race in Ellison's Early Fiction." *College Literature* 29, no. 4 (2002): 109–35.

McKay, Claude. *Harlem Glory: A Fragment of Aframerican Life.* Chicago: Charles H. Kerr, 1990.

McPherson, James Alan. "Indivisible Man." *Atlantic,* December 1970, 45–60.

Morel, Lucas E., ed. *Ralph Ellison and the Raft of Hope: A Political Companion to "Invisible Man."* Lexington: University of Kentucky Press, 2004.

Nadel, Alan. *Invisible Criticism: Ralph Ellison and the American Canon.* Iowa City: University of Iowa Press, 1988.

O'Meally, Robert G. *The Craft of Ralph Ellison.* Cambridge, Mass.: Harvard University Press, 1980.

Podhoretz, Norman. "What Happened to Ralph Ellison." *Commentary,* July–August 1999, 46–58.

Posnock, Ross. *The Cambridge Companion to Ralph Ellison.* Cambridge: Cambridge University Press, 2005.

Rampersad, Arnold. *Ralph Ellison: A Biography.* New York: Alfred A. Knopf, 2007.

Schaub, Thomas Hill. "From Ranter to Writer: Ellison's *Invisible Man* and the New Liberalism." In *American Fiction in the Cold War,* 91–115. Madison: University of Wisconsin Press, 1991.

Singh, Nikhil Pal. *Black Is a Country: Race and the Unfinished Struggle for De-mocracy.* Cambridge, Mass.: Harvard University Press, 2004.

Smethurst, James. "'Something Warmly, Infuriatingly Feminine': Gender, Sexuality and the Work of Ralph Ellison." In *A Historical Guide to Ralph Ellison,* edited by Steven C. Tracy, 115–42. New York: Oxford University Press, 2004.

Stanford, Ann Folwell. "He Speaks for Whom? Inscription and Reinscription of Women in *Invisible Man* and *The Salt Eaters.*" *MELUS* 18, no. 2 (1992): 17–31.

Stephens, Gregory. *On Racial Frontiers: The New Culture of Frederick Doug-lass, Ralph Ellison, and Bob Marley.* Cambridge: Cambridge University Press, 1999.

Sundquist, Eric J. *Cultural Contexts for Ralph Ellison's "Invisible Man."* Bos-ton: Bedford/St. Martin's, 1995.

Tate, Claudia. "Notes on the Invisible Women in Ralph Ellison's *Invisible Man.*" In *Ralph Ellison's Invisible Man: A Casebook,* edited by John F. Callahan, 253–66. New York: Oxford University Press, 2004.

Tracy, Steven C. *A Historical Guide to Ralph Ellison.* New York: Oxford Uni-versity Press, 2004.

Updike, John. "Late Works." *New Yorker,* August 7–14, 2006.

Waniek, Marilyn Nelson. "The Space Where Sex Should Be: Toward a Defini-tion of the Lack American Literary Tradition." *Studies in Black Literature* 6, no. 3 (1975): 7–13.

Warren, Kenneth W. *So Black and Blue: Ralph Ellison and the Occasion of Criticism.* Chicago: University of Chicago Press, 2003.

Warren, Robert Penn. *Who Speaks for the Negro?* New York: Random House, 1965.

Watts, Jerry Gafio. *Heroism and the Black Intellectual: Ralph Ellison, Politics, and Afro American Intellectual Life.* Chapel Hill: University of North Car-olina Press, 1994.

Wershler-Henry, Darren. *The Iron Whim: A Fragmented History of Typewrit-ing.* Ithaca, N.Y.: Cornell University Press, 2005.

West, Cornel. *Democracy Matters: Winning the Fight against Imperialism.* New York: Penguin, 2004.

Winter, Jessica. "It's All in My Head." Slate.com, May 14, 2008.

Wright, John S. *Shadowing Ralph Ellison.* Jackson: University of Mississippi Press, 2006.

Wright, Richard. *Native Son.* New York: Harper, 1940.

———. "Foreword." In George Padmore, *Pan-Africanism or Communism.* 1956. Reprint, New York: Doubleday, 1971.

Acknowledgments

I first read Ralph Ellison's *Invisible Man* as a college freshman in an African-American literature course taught by John F. Callahan. Little did I know at the time just how much my life would be shaped by these two men, the novelist and the professor—one of whom I never met, the other with whom I've since developed a close friendship and deep collaboration through our shared work on Ellison's manuscripts. I am indebted to Professor Callahan for seeing the potential within me as his nineteen-year-old student to assist him in sifting through the mountain of papers that came under his stewardship after he was named Ellison's literary executor. In the years since, I've had the privilege of learning from his fine scholarly example, collaborating with him for more than a decade on editing *Three Days Before the Shooting . . .* , and engaging from time to time in that generative process Ellison liked to call "antagonistic cooperation." I dedicate this book to him in the same way that he once dedicated his book to Ellison—on the *higher* frequencies.

I wish to thank Claremont McKenna College for providing me with a generous research leave, without which this book, too, might have remained forever in progress. I spent that year-

long leave as a visiting fellow at Georgetown University, which
afforded me easy access to Ellison's papers at the Library of
Congress. I wish to acknowledge my new colleagues in the De-
partment of English at the University of Colorado, Boulder,
who offered me the warmest possible welcome to the wintery
Rockies. My belated thanks go to the National Endowment for
the Humanities, which awarded me a Younger Scholars Grant
in the final year of that program's existence for a long essay I
wrote on Ralph Ellison and American identity in my junior
year of college. This book is a culmination of that inquiry,
begun more than fifteen years ago.

I wish to acknowledge the generosity of The Ralph and
Fanny Ellison Charitable trust for permission to reprint portions
of Ellison's unpublished drafts and notes, without which this
book would not have been possible. I owe a debt of gratitude
to everyone at the Library of Congress Manuscripts Division for
their guidance and encouragement over the past dozen years,
especially Dr. Alice Birney for her thoughtful suggestions, as
well as the tremendous group of reference librarians, including
Jennifer Brathovde, Jeffrey Flannery, Joe Jackson, Lia Kerwin,
Patrick Kerwin, and Bruce Kirby.

I am indebted to friends and colleagues who read the
manuscript in draft, especially Lawrence Buell, John Burt,
Robert Faggen, John Farrell, Jeffrey Ferguson, Henry Louis
Gates, Jr., James A. Miller, Werner Sollors, Eric J. Sundquist,
Kenneth W. Warren, John S. Wright, and David Yaffe. My work
has benefited greatly from their comments and challenges.

I've enjoyed rich conversations and correspondence about
Ellison with a number of people over the years, including
Malik Ali, Jabari Asim, Louise Bernard, William Cain, Glenda
Carpio, Marc Conner, Junot Díaz, Roderick A. Ferguson,
Christopher Freeberg, Farah Jasmine Griffin, Michael S. Harper,

R. Scott Heath, Michael Hill, Lena Hill, Jamaica Kincaid, John L. Jackson, Dinaw Mengestu, Lucas Morel, Robert O'Meally, Arnold Rampersad, Ishmael Reed, Robert J. Sawyer, Sheila Walker, and Cornel West. Particular thanks go to Lawrence P. Jackson, who provided me with a model of Ellisonian discipline when I was a graduate student and he was a fellow at the W. E. B. Du Bois Institute at Harvard writing what would become his fine biography of Ellison, *Ralph Ellison: Emergence of Genius*. Thanks to Chris Lydon for many challenging on-air and off-air discussions on all matters Ellison. And thanks to Wil Haygood for writing such a soulful article on Ellison and his posthumous legacy, of which I've been fortunate to play a part.

I thank Robert Guinsler of Sterling Lord Literistic for his tireless support; he is as good a friend as he is an agent. I've had the privilege of working with a stellar editorial team at Yale University Press, from Jonathan Brent, who first took on the project; to Sarah Miller, who saw it through to publication with zeal and skill; to Laura Jones Dooley, who provided meticulous copyediting; and to Sonia Shannon, who designed an elegant jacket.

Finally, I'm thankful for the love of my family, and most of all for the love of my wife, Anna, whose own scholarly example inspires me anew each day.

Index